E-LEARNING:
Expanding
the Training Classroom
through Technology

A COLLECTION OF ARTICLES
BY THE PIONEERS OF E-LEARNING.

EDITED BY LYNNE MEALY AND BOB LOLLER

PREFACE BY TINA SUNG
CEO AND PRESIDENT, ASTD

International
Association for
Human Resource
Information Management

e-learning: *Expanding the Training Classroom through Technology*
A *collection of articles by the pioneers of e-learning*

An IHRIM Book
Published by Rector Duncan & Associates, Inc.
314 Highland Mall Boulevard
Austin, Texas 78752 USA

Table of Contents

■ *E-learning Overview*

■ *E-learning Blueprints*

■ *E-learning Application*

■ *E-learning Issues*

■ *E-learning Future*

Preface

Sons and Daughters of the Pioneers

By Tina Sung
President and CEO, ASTD

Do you know the expression "grow or die?" It's George Land's shorthand for what happens to organisms that reach the culmination of their growth cycle. They either grow by reinventing themselves or they die because they have consumed all the resources that nourished them. Many people believe that education is like an organism that has reached a grow-or-die point and that e-learning bears the seeds of its reincarnation. I agree with that viewpoint.

As the leader of the world's largest organization of learning professionals, I see daily evidence that e-learning is helping reinvent the very fundamentals of the learning process — from instructional design, to the evaluation of results, to who controls the learning experience. Consider some facts about learning today.

The use of the classroom for learning is in decline. One estimate is that by 2003, the traditional classroom model of instruction will represent less than 30 percent of all formal corporate learning programs. Not everyone agrees about the speed or the degree of decline, but there is no ignoring the fact that classroom learning is going to lose its primacy.

In 1999, at the age of 90, the management expert and master teacher Peter Drucker cooperated in putting some of his courses online, proving to me, at least, that he appreciated two of the biggest advantages of e-learning — accessibility and scalability. Even when you are Peter Drucker and the world is beating a path to your classroom, you can only teach so many people there.

When I hear how companies are using e-learning to transform their cultures in weeks instead of years, or to bring a sales force up to earning speed in days instead of months, I add more weight to the e-learning side of the equation.

Big and fast are important, but learning in a business context absolutely must be effective or it will not survive: no executive team will invest in programs that don't product results. ASTD released a report recently showing that a firm's commitment to workplace learning is directly linked to its bottom line. Firms in the top half of our study group who spent more on training had an average total stockholder return of 36.9 percent, while firms in the bottom half had an average TSR of 19.8 percent. For comparison, the S&P 500 had an annual return of 25.5 percent during the same period. In addition, the top-half companies experienced 218 percent higher income per employee.

Not only is an investment in e-learning good for business; e-learning is a good business investment. That is the current view of the entrepreneurs, venture capitalists, and investors who are streaming into the e-learning market in record numbers. In the U.S., the education enterprise, from cradle to grave, is the second largest segment of the economy after healthcare, according to an estimate by the investment firm W.R. Hambrecht and Co.

Not only is an investment in e-learning good for business; e-learning is a good business investment.

So, the pressure is on. CEOs want bottom line results from e-learning. Wall Street wants a return on the millions they are investing in training content, services and infrastructure companies. Managers want learning to produce better performance in their employees. And learners, especially those who've grown up in an e-world, want to be stimulated and challenged by their e-learning experiences. All of us involved in e-learning are partners in a potentially momentous event — the rebirth of learning in the workplace. It's a heady assignment and one that can inspire fear even as it tantalizes, because we are unsure of how to begin.

I have a personal motto from the Spanish poet Machado: "Wanderer, there is no path. You create the path as you walk." The men and women who contributed their ideas to the articles that make up this book are some of the pioneers on the path. And you, because you are reading this book, may be their intellectual sons and daughters on the road to e-learning.

Introduction

BY LYNNE MEALY AND BOB LOLLER

The terms e-business and e-commerce are widely known. And, unless you have been have been living on a deserted island for the last 10 years, you have e-mail or at least know about it. With the advancement of the Internet, you have been exposed to things like e-books and e-auctions. A friend of ours even has an e-pet that lives on his desktop, and if he doesn't feed it regularly, it will e-starve. Isn't it natural that we have e-learning?

What is e-learning? In the articles compiled for this book, you will find that each author has put his or her own spin on the term e-learning, and, regardless of the diversity of definitions, all are correct. Each definition you encounter will accompany facts and experiences that support that author's viewpoint.

Simply speaking, e-learning is the utilization of technology to support the delivery of education.

Simply speaking, e-learning is the utilization of technology to support the delivery of education. E-learning has been around for a long time. It was only recently that we put an "e" in front of it. Twenty years ago, people in the training business were bringing people into training centers, sitting them down in front of a terminal hooked into a large box with headphones, inserting the video disk, and having them spend the next two to three hours (and sometimes longer) learning a new process, product, or program. This was e-learning in its infancy. Students loved it because they could get the training they needed when they wanted it. They didn't have to wait for the next class, which could be months away. The training was available NOW!

Flash forward to today. Internets and intranets deliver the same type of learning directly to a person's workstation so they no longer have to travel to a training center; learning can even be done in the convenience of home 24 hours a day, seven days a week. Streaming video and audio make for a much more enjoyable learning experience. The ability to simulate the environment that the person is learning about provides the practice needed to master the skills. The ability to jump around from topic to topic ensures that the student only needs to take the skill module they need. The ability for students to take classes in desired universities that are geographically distant from them adds flexibility to their learning desires. Companies with locations around the world can do product training from a central location without having to import that field force to that location. These examples only touch the surface of what e-learning is all about and the benefits it brings to universities and corporations.

Some types of training do not lend themselves to online learning (at least not yet).

Does this mean that e-learning will replace the classroom? We don't believe so. People are social creatures; there will always be a desire to get together with others to share learning experiences. The desire to watch someone else make the same mistakes as you in a training class is only human nature; remember, "misery loves company." And vice versa — when a student finally catches on to an idea they are being taught, don't they like their colleagues to see the light bulb go off over their head? Some types of training do not lend themselves to online learning (at least not yet). But there is a place for e-learning in any learning institution, whether it is the corporate office or the university. Throughout this book you will see examples of how classroom and e-learning are successfully integrated to create a total learning experience.

Having been in the education business for several years, we have seen our share of e-learning initiatives come and go. Some have been successful and others have failed, but not because the concept doesn't work. There are many variables, roadblocks and obstacles encountered when implementing an e-learning program. Just like any project, the concept has to be well thought out, a cost benefit done, implementation plans developed, product assessment performed, evaluations made, test criteria established, marketing and communication plans put in place and so on. You all know the drill. This book will help you understand what is needed to do all this and more. Large companies, medium size companies, and even small companies can benefit by incorporating components of e-learning into their education strategy. To what degree these components need to be incorporated depend on the company's education initiatives.

But in order to assess that, you first need to understand what e-learning is, its capabilities and its benefits — and this book will help you do that.

This book is a collection of articles, stories, and case studies from some of the leading pioneers in the field of e-learning. We have attempted to present their findings in a logical order, from overview concepts through implementation and beyond. There are articles from practitioners, academia, vendors, consultants and "gurus" in the field of e-learning. Topics covered include designing e-learning applications, developing content, cost justification, e-learning principles, corporate universities, online testing and evaluation, privacy issues and lessons learned. Special thanks to ASTD (the American Society for Training and Development) for providing the preface for this book.

We all have a lot to learn. Hopefully this book will get you on your way. If you are just beginning to explore e-learning, there is material that will get you started. If you have been working in the field for a while, there is material that will add to your knowledge base. In fact, we're willing to bet that even if you are an expert in the field, there is material that will cause one or two "ah-ha's." We should never stop learning, or make that we never stop e-learning!

Lynne Mealy
Chief Knowledge Officer
IHRIM

Bob Loller
Vice-Chair IHRIM
AVP, *Training and Development*
Phoenix Home Life Mutual Insurance Company

■ *Post script from Bob Loller:*

Even though I have spent a good portion of my professional career dealing with employee development, something happened the other night that reminded me again of how little we often associate actual events to the careers we live and breathe. My son was having a tough time remembering what his science homework was. Being an astute user of the Internet (i.e. I surf a lot), I decided that we would check the web site for his school and see if the homework assignment was posted. Not only was the homework posted, but also study guides

Talk about being hit over the head with the e-learning stick.

for help in doing that homework, future assignments and reference links to allow students to explore additional material on the subjects being taught. Certainly a far cry from when I was a student. I then offered to print the study guides for him and he looked at me with an expression of disbelief and said simply, "Dad, they are on the Internet, and when I need them I will get on and look at them. Printing them would be a waste of paper." Talk about being hit over the head with the e-learning stick. (Of course, if my boss should read this, I will emphatically deny any of that happened.)

E-learning Overview

Chapter 1
Distance Education:
Closer Than You Think!

By John G. Kelly, CEBS

As we move more towards a knowledge-based workforce, the need for life-long learning is becoming more obvious. As companies struggle to attract and retain key resources, developing a knowledge management strategy and executing on that strategy is critical. Distance education is one important component in many of the tactical plans.

Higher education does not embrace change quickly enough. But, a combination of technological, demographic and societal changes is providing the impetus for a major paradigm shift in education.

As education shifts, there will not be the opportunity to continue to build "brick and mortar" campuses to serve every emerging need. At least part of the learning process will need to utilize technology as a key component for future education delivery.

■ *What is Distance Education?*

Distance Education (DE) is the process of providing education where the instruction and the learning are in different physical locations. DE has been around for a long time. Historically, it took the form of correspondence courses. Materials would be mailed to students who would complete readings, reports and exams.

Figure I. Paradigm Shift in Education.

"As-Is"	"Expected-to-Be" (In 5-10 years)
◆ 16 million students	◆ 100 million learners
◆ Teacher-centric	◆ Student-centric
◆ Provider-driven	◆ Individualized learning
◆ Time out for education	◆ Perpetual learning

With the advent of TV, videotaping and satellite broadcasting, distance education expanded beyond textbooks. Using these technologies, learners could achieve a classroom-like experience without physically attending class. While these efforts were advancements over paper-based approaches, they generally required expensive production environments.

The Internet has added several other important dimensions to DE.

The Computer-Based Training (CBT) technologies that evolved in the 1980s used the *de facto* PC standard that existed. Multimedia technology at the time was often hardware dependent and expensive. Development tools were primitive, and the resulting costs were such that this technology was not widely adopted. In addition, software distribution often required the physical distribution of CDs or other media, and updating content was problematic.

The Internet has added several other important dimensions to DE. It has provided a low-cost distribution mechanism for content delivery, a common operating system for multiple hardware platforms and a potentially cost-effective development environment.

◼ Distributed Learning (DL)

Distance Education is also referred to by other terms such as "just-in-time learning," "virtual learning," "Internet-based training" and e-learning. The emerging term for the range of approaches associated with DE is "Distributed Learning" (DL) which encompasses not only students at a distance, but also learners that utilize technology to enhance the learning experience locally.

■ Synchronous Learning

In synchronous learning, students are taught at the same time (although not necessary at the same place). A common example of synchronous learning is when a course is video broadcast to several different sites to be viewed at the same time. This can be accomplished via microwave (for local) and satellite (for greater distances) transmission.

This approach has the advantage of keeping the students grouped together throughout the learning program. Typically, students can ask questions interactively (via conferencing facilities) and they benefit from interacting in the context of the classroom setting.

■ Asynchronous Learning

Asynchronous learning occurs when the students are learning independently and not necessarily on the same schedule with other students. While this has occurred since the early days of correspondence courses, the advent of CBT and Web-based learning has greatly reduced the feedback cycle necessary for effective learning.

■ Non-Linear Instruction

One of the key advantages of using a technology-based approach to providing DE is that it provides a framework for self-paced learning. A student is not required to take a course at a pace slower or faster than necessary. In a traditional class setting, learning occurs at a rate slightly below the average for the class. Many students who could move ahead faster are constrained by slow learners in the class.

Non-linear instruction allows learners to access instruction in the order best suited for their needs. With proper design, DE courses can be developed so students take only the portions of the course about which they don't already know the required content. Pretests and ongoing assessments direct material to learners in the appropriate order. This approach reduces learning time and provides better feedback for overcoming learning deficiencies.

■ Key Technologies for Distance Education

The distance education process introduces a number of new technologies. Some of these technologies are well established (such as e-mail), while other technologies still await advances in the Internet infrastructure to fully achieve their promise (e.g., video streaming).

■ E-mail

E-mail has been around for a while, and its use is often integral to DE courses. E-mail provides a high-speed conduit from learner to teacher. In many cases, time and space may separate the teacher from the learner. E-mail provides the mechanism to ask questions, receive answers, provide supplemental information and support materials, and distribute and collect assignments.

■ Electronic Chat Rooms

Electronic chat rooms enable students to collaborate on projects and exchange information. These discussions can be mediated by an instructor or unmediated. E-chat rooms are more effective for synchronous courses or courses where the students move through the course material at approximately the same pace. In "open semester" courses (no specific starting date or ending date), e-chats are more difficult since not all the students are at the same place in the learning process. For very large programs or courses, e-chats can be an effective way to encourage interaction between students.

■ Message Boards

Message boards or posting boards provide another avenue for student information exchange. This approach does not require students to be online at the same instant. Students can post comments, questions and answers on a continual basis. These message boards often provide an excellent source of frequently asked questions (FAQs) on course materials. In many cases, message boards will be more useful than e-chat rooms.

■ Audio Streaming

The process of broadcasting audio over the Web has come a long way in the last few years. Connection speeds and new software (plug-ins for browsers) have made the use of audio in courses practical. Audio streaming can be on a real-time basis or on demand. Speed will still be a consideration. Most applications will require 28.8K or 57K modems.

■ Video Streaming

Video streaming, or broadcasting moving video over the Web, also has improved over the last couple of years. The quality has suffered since the speed to transmit smooth full-motion video is not available to most remote users. In facilities with high-speed lines (T-1s) or cable modems, transmission can be of much higher quality. Video streaming provides the bridge from the prior video broadcast or videotaped technology of the 1980s. Increased transmission speeds will greatly improve the effectiveness of DE in general.

■ Approaches to Distance Education

Studies indicate that it takes knowledge workers the equivalent of seven credit hours per year to maintain their current positions. Corporations have to make decisions on how to meet these learning needs.

■ In-house Developed Courses

Corporations that have unique training requirements often choose to develop materials internally. This may especially be true when the training materials must be constantly updated to reflect new knowledge. If the training provides key business advantages, it may also be developed internally to provide a competitive business advantage (e.g., specific sales training, software development methodologies).

One of the critical requirements will be the acquisition of effective course development tools. While it is possible to develop courses using basic HTML, the cost of maintaining these materials over time suggests that purchasing a course development tool would be desirable. There are a number of Web-based tools in the marketplace, and each has its unique set of advantages and disadvantages. Some important selection criteria include:

➤ compliance with IMS standard (discussed later in this article),

➤ support of various media (video, graphics, audio, etc.),

➤ potential for "non-linear" instruction,

➤ cost of delivery (are end-user licenses required?), and

➤ support for multiple browsers.

■ Purchased Courses

In some cases, it is more cost-effective to purchase courses from a vendor or educational organization. The most frequently purchased courses are for general training (e.g., business communications, presentation skills, word processing, spreadsheets, etc.). Since many of these courses are mass-produced, the per-unit cost is generally lower, and the quality (theoretically) should be better. Some important selection criteria are:

➤ compliance with IMS standards (discussed later in this article),

➤ support of various media (video, graphics, audio, etc.),

➤ content quality (compared to specific needs),

➤ cost per use (licensing arrangements),

➤ cost and implementation of training updates, and

➤ support for multiple browsers.

■ Co-developed Education

It is becoming increasingly popular for corporations to work in cooperation with colleges and universities to develop content customized for a company's culture and unique business requirements. These arrangements are particularly useful because they draw on strengths from both industry and higher education. In developing these partnerships, you should consider:

➤ flexibility in delivery approaches (video conferencing, Web-based, etc.),

➤ access for remote sites,

➤ updating of course content over time,

➤ up-front development costs and ongoing support costs, and

➤ delivery time frame.

■ Outsourced Education

Traditionally, a significant portion of corporate learning was outsourced to colleges and universities or specialty vendors. Small- and medium-sized employers continue to be dependent on this approach, and, in the future, they may outsource the management of the training process to vendors or institutions as well. Companies may identify specific skills and core competencies and engage a third party to manage the entire training function including the selection of vendors, assessment and tracking. In selecting an outsourcing vendor, you should consider:

➤ flexibility (multiple vendor relationships),

➤ purchasing power,

➤ the ability to integrate course content from multiple sources

➤ up-front setup costs and ongoing support costs, and

➤ the ability to match core competencies and skills required with training opportunities.

■ *Challenges in Distance Education*

As DE evolves, a number of obstacles need to be overcome. Some require technological improvements; others demand process and cultural changes.

Managing asynchronous courses: It is difficult to manage classes where students are moving through materials at different rates. Taking advantage of nonlinear learning, some learners may not cover the material completely. Underlying management systems are critical in tracking the learners' progress. Teachers need to adjust to mentoring students at different stages at the same time.

➤ *Developing courses to fully utilize the interactive potential of the Web*: When cars were first introduced, they had reins like horse-drawn carriages. The steering wheel came later as a better way to steer this new invention. Frequently, courses are transferred to the Web from their text/class-based origins. In some cases, the class notes, lecture slides and homework/reading assignments are posted on a Web page. This approach limits the potential for fully achieving an interactive experience. While these initial steps are important, instructors need to use interactive design concepts to take full advantage of the Web's potential as a learning tool.

➤ *Managing course completion*: While students are in a synchronous class environment, they are encouraged to move through the course materials at a pace that achieves course completion over a specified period of time (commonly a semester). With self-paced learning available though DE, a learner can extend the learn-

Useful Web Pages and Links

You can access these and other links via www.sctcorp.com\DE.

Web Page	Description
www.imsproject.org	The IMS project Web page
www.maise.com/	The Maise Center
www.uwex.edu/disted/home.html	Distance Education Clearinghouse
www.filename.com/wbt/index.html	Web-based Training Information Center
http://sqzm14.ust.hk/distance/ evolution-distance-learning.htm	The Evolution of Distance Learning (by Edward F. Spodick)
www.itta.org/	Information Technology Training Association
www.trainingmedia.org/	Training Media Association
www.detc.org/	The Distance and Education Training Council
www.ed.psu.edu/acsde/	The American Center for the Study of Distance Education
http://idl.fsu.edu/	The Center for Academic Support and Distance Education

ing process longer than the traditional period. While this provides advantages to students with competing time commitments, it can also delay course completion, or in some cases, defer it indefinitely.

➤ *Intellectual Property*: Once the course material is produced, who owns it? Most private companies have patent and copyright conditions as part of the employment agreement. As companies work with course developers, vendors and outsourcing partners, the issue becomes potentially more complex. This is especially true in higher education. Most education organizations are only now addressing some of the legal ramifications of new media and intellectual property rights.

➤ *Assessment*: When a student attends a course in person and takes a proctored exam, there is a high comfort level in the assessment results. In DE, when students may not attend physical classes, there is concern that the assessment process may not be secure enough. As a result, some programs require exams to be taken onsite or at a proctored center (Sylvan Learning Centers, local colleges, divisional work locations, etc.). New biometric devices may also become practical in the next five to 10 years. (Biometric devices rely on unique physical characteristics of an individual to establish identity such as finger prints, retina patterns, hand geometry, etc.)

➤ *End-User Support*: While the Web is a standard way of delivering materials for DE, there is a need to support users with various PCs, browsers, ISPs (Internet Service Providers) and operating systems. This can require substantial support services. Since learners can often choose to study at various times, support coverage needs to be 24 hours a day, seven days a week, 52 weeks a year. Most companies and higher education providers are not ready for this commitment.

■ Instructional Management Systems (IMS)

In November 1994, EDUCAUSE — with offices in Washington, D.C. and Boulder, Colorado — launched a new initiative called the National Learning Infrastructure Initiative (NLII). The NLII identified a common need among educational institutions for a non-proprietary, Internet-based Instructional Management System (IMS) to provide the means to customize and manage the instructional process and to integrate content from multiple publishers in distributed or virtual learning environments. The IMS project is developing and promoting open specifications for facilitating online activities such as locating and using educational content, tracking learner progress, reporting learner performance and exchanging student records between administrative systems. These specifications will increase the range of distributed learning opportunities, and it is hoped that they will promote the creativity and productivity of both teachers and learners.

Unfortunately, the development of the IMS standards is not proceeding at a pace comparable to the rate of change of the Internet.

Overall, the IMS project attempts to address three obstacles for providing effective online materials and learning environments:

➤ the lack of standards for locating and operating interactive platform-independent materials,

➤ the lack of support for the collaborative and dynamic nature of learning, and

➤ the lack of incentives and structure for developing and sharing content.

What is needed to address the obstacles described above is a specific set of higher-order standards and tools that enable teachers, learners, software developers, content providers and other parties involved in the learning process to create, manage and access the use of online learning materials and environments. The IMS is this set of standards and tools. Unfortunately, the development of the IMS standards is not proceeding at a pace comparable to the rate of change of the Internet. As companies move forward with their efforts in DE, some consideration should be given to these emerging standards.

■ Distance Education and Human Resources

Human Resources needs to focus on using DE to maximize its effectiveness. It may not be cost-effective in every case, and it may not be appropriate for certain activities. (We would not want to visit a physician who learned about a surgical procedure strictly from an online course on the Web, would we?) There are clearly some key opportunities for HR in DE.

■ Attenuation

In attenuation courses (transferrable credit) taught in a corporate setting, learners can receive college credit for degree purposes. Schools such as the University of Phoenix and Thomas Edison College have been aggressive at working with business to promote this approach.

■ Corporate Partnerships with Higher Education

Working with higher education remains key to utilizing DE for many companies. Higher education's mission is delivering knowledge. Institutions of higher education have competencies in teaching and course design development, and, in many cases, they also have the technology infrastructure to generate the necessary leverage — by serving multiple organizations — to make DE cost-effective.

It is critical for corporations and higher education to work together to develop programs that deliver necessary skills and knowledge on demand. Colleges and universities need to design custom content to reflect the specific needs of particular industries and markets.

■ *Bridge to Knowledge Management (KM)*

As we move forward into the next millennium, corporations will move beyond training and need to focus on managing knowledge throughout the organization. The technologies introduced in DE can have a profound effect on this process. Adding and preserving knowledge will be a key component to successful companies in the future. Fortunately, the technology seeds are being planted today!

Source:John G. Kelly, "Distance Education: Closer Than You Think!," IHRIM.link, February/March 1999, pp. 14-22.

Chapter 2
E-learning Overview

By Anita Rosen

New technologies such as the Internet and changing business practices such as the use of more consultants are modifying the way we work. Our current low unemployment rate is making hiring a challenge at every level. Companies, especially those in competitive sectors, will need to use training as one of their most powerful tools. It increases employee productivity, builds stronger and more effective relationships with business partners, and creates greater brand awareness/preference with customers. Training has moved to a critical role because companies need to maintain their competitive edge

Training needs in the corporate world are definitely growing, and companies need to find ways to make their training more efficient. Traditional classroom training is still a very effective method primarily because it is interactive, and it provides a structured environment that encourages for students to complete the courses. However, classroom training has several drawbacks: high cost and difficulty of student access. Arranging for employees located in different facilities to be in the same room at the same time can be very difficult and expensive.

To get around these negatives, companies have provided employees with books and CD-based courses. Books are easy to use, but it is nearly impossible to keep busy employees focused on learning from them — books do not provide any interactivity or methods to force the student to complete the course. It is also very difficult to maintain a book's timeliness. CD-based courses are better because they can include interactive exercises. However, just as books, they are difficult to keep current and they provide low impetus for course completion. Both CD's and books are also expensive to distribute. These limitations force companies to look for methods that are low cost, effective, interactive, accessible, and motivational. E-learning has stepped in as the latest approach to solve the employee training problem.

E-learning is best defined as the category consisting of training and learning over the Web — training that can be delivered over an intranet, extranet or the Internet. Since courses can be centrally administrated, it's easy to track students (thereby providing motivation to complete courses), control content (for easy updates as material changes) and inexpensive to deploy (since distribution of media is not an issue). Students can access training from their desktop.

There are two popular forms of e-learning: asynchronous and synchronous learning. Asynchronous consists of learning that is stand-alone and can be delivered through the Web, via an intranet, or an extranet. The main feature is that the student takes courses when it is convenient for them. In contrast, synchronous e-learning is carried out at designated dates and times. Delivery is through the Web, so that an instructor can take advantage of new technologies such as electronic presentation delivery, chat sessions and collaborative electronic blackboards. Essentially, the concept of classroom training is extended to distance learning through the use of technology.

Studies have shown that with instructor-led e-learning, students finish courses 90 times faster than through stand-alone training.

Studies have shown that with instructor-led e-learning, students finish courses 90 times faster than through stand-alone training. Instructor-led training provides the impetus for completion traditionally found in classroom training. Stand-alone training, augmented by an electronically available tutor, provides a blend of asynchronous and synchronous training.

In today's market there are three main categories of e-learning products and services:

1. Corporate learning management systems (LMSs);

2. E-learning training portals; and

3. Authoring tools.

These three categories, in most cases, complement each other. Corporate LMSs are software/hardware combinations that host and manage courses, and monitor employee progress. They are usually accessed by the employee through a company's intranet. Many companies have decided not to host courses within their company but to work with an e-Learning training portal. E-learning portals are training web sites accessible via the Internet where courses are served. They usually include a learning management system, and may include asynchronous and/or synchronous environments. The third category for e-learning is Authoring tools. Authoring tools are software used to create training courses. It is estimated that 80 percent of all corporate training is produced within the company. Content experts can use an e-Learning-authoring tool to turn corporate information into an e-Learning course that can then be hosted on their web site, in an internal LMS or through a portal.

Whichever e-learning route a company chooses, they should be aware that the more complex the training environment the more expensive it will be to serve and support (increasing complexity = increasing costs). It is easy to get caught-up in the enthusiasm of new technology and fancy graphics. The fundamental question that companies should be asking when they decide to invest in e-learning is "Where will content be obtained?" After all, a fancy learning environment without any content is useless.

Most generic training courses have already been produced and can be found on a number of e-learning portal sites. Corporate e-learning is most effective when companies can focus on courses that are specific to their products/services. The goal is to inexpensively and quickly provide employees with access to the latest information. There are several options to produce custom training: hire an outside Web training company to develop courses, hire technical developers to port existing content to a Web format, or purchase a tool that content experts and classroom trainers can use to create their own courses.

> *Corporate e-learning is most effective when companies can focus on courses that are specific to their products/services.*

Until recently, there were no tools available that the content experts (as opposed to the power users) could easily use. Now that they are available, there are several issues that should be considered. First, identify the up front costs and cost to develop the training. An important aspect to consider is the trainer's ability to use the environment. A tool that provides trainers with powerful capabilities but takes weeks to learn will most likely not provide a productivity gain. Also, consider:

➤ The learning curve — how many days of training is required to start using the tool?

➤ Ability to pour current material into training environment — can material in formats such as Microsoft PowerPoint™ be poured into your e-learning tool?

➤ Is pedagogy inherent in training environment — will you need to hire a team of professional course designers to create training?

➤ Ease of deployment — will courses produced run easily on your network?

Even large networks can easily be overwhelmed by traffic from heavy graphics. It is best to keep Web-enabled applications simple and small so students don't get frustrated. Good graphics are those that help a student learn. The goal is to provide an effective learning environment, not to produce prize-winning videos and graphics. Additionally, consider the needs of supporting students working outside the corporate offices, at partner sites or over the Internet. Courses that can be deployed to the widest possible market will be used the most, and will provide the greatest return on investment. Due to corporate firewalls, most partner and customer environments will not accept courses deployed using specialized plug-ins or macros. This eliminates many types of graphics like video and audio. The best choices are simple courses built as standard Web pages.

In conclusion, online training is being used in the corporate world to save money, to provide employees with easy access to information and to extend the reach of trainers.

Chapter 3
E-learning:
The Business Imperative

By Brandon Hall

Faced with broad-based and growing challenges related to providing sufficient opportunities for employees to stay current and competent in their jobs, organizations are turning confidently to e-learning to provide wider and faster access to rich training and information. Learning is now recognized as a highly strategic process and an engine of organizational performance — a necessary expense.

Brandon-hall.com has conducted an intensive research study examining eleven domestic and international companies that have implemented e-learning on a significant level. This study, called "Benchmarking: E-Learning Across the Enterprise," describes the strategies and experiences of these organizations, and how they overcame challenges to implement e-learning successfully.

■ Bringing More Learning to More People, Faster, Anytime, Anywhere, at Less Cost

Why are best-practice organizations implementing e-learning on an enterprise-wide scale? The U. S. Navy says it most succinctly: it's about "getting more training to more sailors, anytime, anywhere, at less cost."

Overall, when organizations were asked to state their top reasons for moving to e-learning, meat-and-potatoes business reasons (e.g., faster access, lower

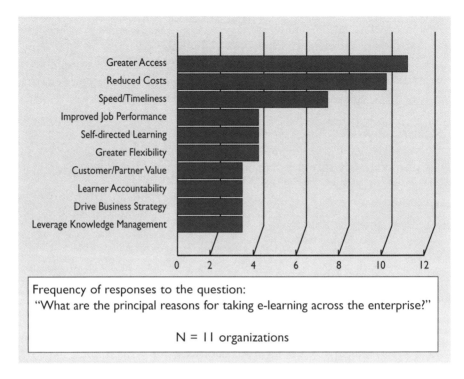

Frequency of responses to the question:
"What are the principal reasons for taking e-learning across the enterprise?"

N = 11 organizations

costs, speed of training) overshadowed reasons closer to the hearts of training professionals (such as performance, flexibility, accountability), which are further removed from the bottom line.

■ What do Managers Really Want?

Best-practice organizations are implementing e-learning aggressively and with a focus on their biggest training and learning challenges — because of rapid growth and limited accessibility of training, much specialized training was not being done in some organizations. Benefits in the form of cost savings are very encouraging.

While proponents of e-learning may worry about a wide range of metrics, top management in some organizations is more impressed with faster-moving information and on-the-job learning that eliminates training backfill costs, than with any measures of effectiveness. This is a good thing because, in one participant's estimation, it will take about two years of tracking to identify trends and to quantify results that can be attributed to the e-learning intervention.

While the business imperative is very strong — Shell claims that "no alternative to e-learning is being considered" — costs are only one part of the story.

Best-practice organizations are moving from a perception of learning as a cost to one of learning to maximize value. This leads to increasing demand for skills and knowledge delivered in a much shorter cycle time — in short, a greater demand for access and speed.

Organizations are taking a phased approach to e-learning, taking care to ensure the sustainability of the implementation. Since e-learning scales so well and is supported by such a strong business imperative, constant evolution is maintained. In advanced implementations, e-learning is intertwined with the fabric of the enterprise.

■ From Learning as Cost to Learning as Revenue Source: Extending E-Learning Beyond the Enterprise

Several other organizations agree with Cisco that Adding Customer/Partner Value is a key reason for e-learning. IBM, Ernst & Young, Verizon, Unipart and Air Canada all offer e-learning products and services to their customers and/or partners. This is a logical strategy for:

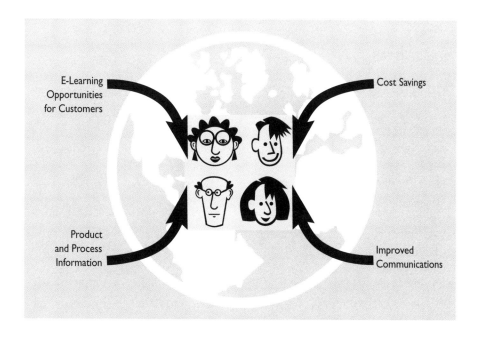

➤ Creating a revenue stream from strategies, methods and technologies developed in the course of the internal e-learning implementation,

➤ Adding value to complex products and services,

➤ Helping to pay for the development of custom content, via external sales, and

➤ Shifting some of the information and learning load to customers, thereby allowing sales and support staff to focus on more complex products and problems.

■ E-Learning as a Driver for E-Culture

For three organizations, a key reason for e-learning is to drive business strategy — they see it as a key driver and enabler of business "e-culture," because it has the greatest power to engage employees in the overall e-business strategy and transformation. Cisco advises that "trying to make the transition to e-business is impossible until you develop an e-culture. The best way to enable an e-culture is through e-learning."

■ At-Home Learning: Too Much of a Good Thing?

While this concern is not new, e-learning amplifies the risk of employees doing training on their own time and at their own expense. While this may appear to be a great financial windfall from e-learning, almost all participating organizations take a long-term view of this "Trojan horse" issue, preferring to explicitly allocate training time and, when necessary, compensating employees for learning done outside of business hours.

For organizations like the U. S. Navy, one of e-learning's key advantages is improving retention by reducing the amount of time trainees spend away from their families. Expecting personnel to pay for this increased quality time out of their own pockets would make little sense. Ernst & Young —where average employee tenure is 4.25 years, and 2,500 people join the company each year — is of the same mind on this issue, seeing the improved work-life balance that's made possible by e-learning as a competitive recruiting and retention advantage.

Senior management's strong leadership and close involvement with the e-learning implementation are keys to its success, and are being offered with little or no resistance. Broad-based Learning Councils, or otherwise-named steering committees, are standard practice to keep developments aligned and on track.

■ Big-Time Cost Savings

"With a traditional model of leader-led courses, training 5,000 staff members ten days a year would cost over US$40 million in annual travel, classroom and instructor costs. This is unacceptable and not scalable, and the pace will only increase." (Cisco Systems — whose goal is to reduce field training costs by 50 percent with e-learning.)

As far as costs are concerned, e-learning is a big winner. This is not surprising since, as one organization puts it, "one-half the cost of classroom training is just getting trainees in the room!" Virtually all organizations far enough along to be measuring cost savings/avoidance and ROI report positive results. (In the graph, "Unknown" results are mostly due to implementations being in too early a stage for detailed data to be available.)

Reduced training time is reported to be a significant component of e-learning savings, and as the proportion of training delivered via e-learning rises, to-

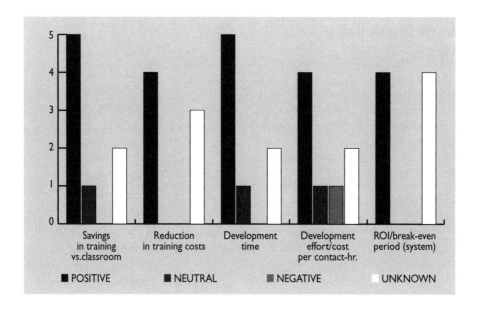

tal training time could be seen to drop in some organizations. This has been the case at Ernst & Young, where employees using e-learning find themselves spending on average 55 hours per year in learning activities, as opposed to 70 hours previously, but reportedly with greater overall effectiveness. Others say the opposite is happening because, as learning becomes more readily accessible, more people are spending more time learning, regardless of higher e-learning efficiencies.

> *An e-learning*
> *implementation is*
> *as difficult,*
> *if not as costly,*
> *as an ERP implementation;*
> *it took some organizations*
> *eight or nine years*
> *to get to where*
> *they are today.*

Either way, corporate policies of the "40 hours of training per year" variety may need to be revised or eliminated altogether, in favor of competency management strategies.

Reported savings in development time and cost may appear surprising given the higher complexity of e-learning development when compared to classroom training. Nonetheless, the organizations in question are also the ones using reusable learning object strategies, and they are confident that overall deployment times, from design to delivery, are indeed dropping. In one case, savings in development time were reported in a context where existing content was being converted to e-learning, rather than being developed from scratch.

■ *The Importance of Sustainability*

An e-learning implementation is as difficult, if not as costly, as an ERP implementation; it took some organizations eight or nine years to get to where they are today. Accordingly, best practice organizations invest significantly in planning and strategic development. While these organizations have often had to reinvent plans and strategies along the way, they have cut a number of alternative paths for others to follow.

While no generic plan emerges — Rockwell Collins and others caution that each organization's e-learning plan will be very specific to its own context — all organizations show deep concern for sustainability. Air Canada, for instance, recognized its personnel and expertise constraints, and opted for an implementation focused on ramp employees, a group with important learning needs and access problems. Their advice is simple: "Go too quickly/broadly, and you risk making promises you can't keep! Go too slowly/narrowly, and you risk anonymity." Also critical is realizing that the speed with which e-learning can be rolled out is clearly dependent on organizational culture and readiness.

Unipart confirms the critical importance of sustainability. Still in the relatively early stages of its e-learning implementation, it has opted for simple technologies and designs in the early stages in order to ensure success. "Ignore this at your peril," Unipart warns, "People reverse-engineer change routinely!" For its part, Verizon Learning Systems made sure its phased implementation plan was consistent with the organization's adoption rate for new technology.

Each stage of the IRS's e-learning evolution also began with small, independent projects used to demonstrate success and to gain support for expanding to the entire enterprise with the necessary infrastructure. Demonstration projects, accomplished with a localized infrastructure, allowed different groups to realize that they had the same needs for a national infrastructure to support e-learning.

All of the organizations studied had substantial plans for the future of their e-learning implementations — expanding access, enriching offerings and tackling tougher competence and business problems. More like e-commerce than technology implementation, e-learning implementations are on-going and begin generating benefits early on. Follow Cisco's advice: "Don't strive for perfection; focus first on key learner needs which can be addressed relatively quickly, and plan to enhance (your) portal every 60 to 90 days."

While implementations are evolutionary, some organizations like Air Canada note the key impact of a fundamental change in paradigm or revelation along the way. For Unipart, it was about the almost boundless synergy between knowledge management and e-learning.

■ *Senior Bosses Like E-Learning*

Strategies to educate stakeholders and integrate with other enterprise-wide initiatives are most frequently cited as essential.

Given the very substantial business imperative and business impact of e-learning, it is not surprising that the extent of executive-level support and involvement is high among most best-practice organizations. As IBM says simply, senior management "supports e-learning because it delivers what is needed, when it is needed."

At Cisco, for instance, CEO John Chambers began by stating early on that e-learning was the "next big killer application," and that it would determine an or-

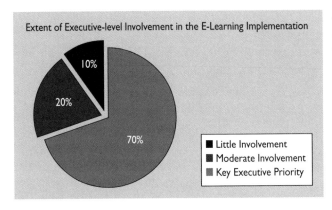

Extent of Executive-level Involvement in the E-Learning Implementation

10%

20%

70%

■ Little Involvement
■ Moderate Involvement
■ Key Executive Priority

ganization's success and competitive advantage. This reportedly led to reactions on the part of many people in the company and in the industry. Senior management across the company quickly got on board, stating that they were going to focus on e-learning, and integrate into their objectives that 50 percent of all education would be conducted through e-learning. More recently, Chambers approved and launched a US$20 million ad campaign for the company's national TV commercials, which promote e-learning with the theme "Are you ready?"

Admiral Crane, the Navy's Chief of Education and Training, is also a champion of e-learning; the Navy Learning Network is his top priority for this year. In organizations where it is traditionally very tough to get regional and unit managers all on board for corporate-wide initiatives, it is reported that e-learning is a shining exception.

Indeed, e-learning is a pretty easy sell at the top. Accordingly, Unipart warns that most "anchor draggers" needing to be dealt with are at middle management level, not at the top.

Learning and training are at last comfortably seated at the big table. Beyond a mere source of cost benefits, organizations are seeing e-learning as a major component of their drive to have a competent and flexible workforce, and to optimize their intellectual capital, retain their people, and ensure long-term viability of the enterprise in a sea of change.

To overcome common sources of resistance and ensure that all stakeholders understand the personal and organizational benefits of e-learning, best practice organizations are unleashing a creative and effective variety of communications and "selling" strategies, each crafted for a specific audience.

■ Competency Management

The majority of participating organizations have implemented competency management, individualized, Web-enabled curriculum maps or learning profiles based on job analyses, as a fundamental element and even key driver of their e-learning system.

By placing part of the responsibility in employees' hands and rewarding them for learning and evolving, competency management accelerates the penetration of e-learning. As Cisco claims, "with e-learning you can empower the learner — the student becomes a knowledge broker, and therefore a power broker. The learner, as well as the mentoring system, is held accountable." Shell implements this principle via an open resource system for job assignments — individuals must market themselves internally and understand that they get the job if they have the competencies. Accreditation provides further motivation. Ernst & Young has similarly adopted a self-service model where it is "the employees' responsibility to make themselves employable." However, it claims that certain policing mechanisms remain necessary to ensure consistency in learning and competency development; it is hoped that within a decade, all learning will be employee-controlled.

While at least one organization had difficulty mapping out competencies for some less well defined jobs — calling these "Jell-O jobs" — most have invested heavily in the effort. Cisco, for instance, created twelve new specialization tracks (areas of technology expertise) for field systems engineers, implementing these in eight months for the Field E-Learning Connection. Roadmaps were developed by a cross-functional team from across the organization, and approved by representatives from the field and from management.

Several organizations make the logical link between mapping competencies and mapping organizational processes. They note the importance of being process-driven first, and eliminating non-value-added work, before investing heavily in knowledge creation and dissemination. Others note the growing importance of considering future learning needs explicitly in the business plan, of integrating competencies into long-term plans. Ernst & Young addresses still another key issue — attempting to integrate team and organizational performance into its competency management vision.

Top Management's Level of Confidence that the E-Learning Initiative Is Effective

0%

20%

80%

■ Very High
■ Moderate
■ Low

The research report also discusses tactics and models utilized by these organizations, methods of incorporating the types of content they want and need, and the tools they used to put these methods and tactics into effect. A reproducible e-learning model emerges, which is a highly compatible threesome, uniting:

➤ Online learning for information transfer and procedural skill acquisition, complemented as necessary by performance support and e-collaboration. This strategy of having learners do pre-work online has gained full acceptance in most participating organizations.

➤ Classroom or other site-based learning for higher order competencies, complemented as required by sophisticated simulation tools.

➤ Structured on-the-job learning, integrating expert mentoring, knowledge banks, other knowledge management resources, and competency or performance evaluation.

■ Summary

The Benchmarking Study identifies best practices in large-scale implementations, at different stages of evolution. It documents state-of-the-art execution of enterprise-wide e-learning, and describes the strategies and experiences of these organizations and how they have overcome challenges to implement e-learning successfully. The organizations highlighted are a reflection of business today — they cover a wide range of industries, contexts, e-learning needs, cultures, and markets. The Best Practices Survey used to provide the background for this study was designed to measure the efficiency and progress of e-learning throughout different types of organizations, as well as to pinpoint weaknesses and potential drawbacks, in an attempt to further define the e-learning industry.

Editor's Note: The Benchmarking Study was sponsored by Cisco Systems, Eastman Kodak, IBM, Miller Brewing, Motorola University and NCR.

Chapter 4
The Foundation of Effective E-learning Strategies —

Performance and Results

By Thomas J. Falkowski

■ Today's Reality

Virtually every organization in today's economy is under incredible pressure. It is no longer acceptable to maintain the status quo. No matter what the business or industry, the pressure is there. Whether it is to expand market share, globalize, innovate, add new products and services, improve productivity, diversify, consolidate or just simply to beat the competition, the charge is the same; "we must improve our performance, we must get results . . . nothing else is acceptable."

After literally decades of espousing that people are our most important asset, companies are beginning to believe their own rhetoric. The resources and assets that made organizations successful in the industrial age are not sufficient today. The new millennium is finally bringing with it the dawn of the information age that has been struggling to blossom over the last two decades. Real estate, raw materials and capital equipment are no longer the only critical resources; intellectual capital is the key to success.

Leading organizations are looking to use learning technologies to help people capture, configure, distribute and leverage their intellectual capital in ways never before possible providing virtually unlimited reach and scalability.

■ Unrealized Potential

This pressing organizational requirement to leverage intellectual capital has transformed the need for learning from a nice to have but inconvenient distraction from the real job, to a strategy that is central to growth and ultimately to survival of organizations. This has turned things upside down in organizations. Some human resources and training organizations are finding themselves out of their element and unprepared to respond. In many organizations, line managers are taking things into their own hands and trying to drive training activities at the department level bypassing the perceived training bureaucracy. While these efforts achieve results, they often fall short of expectations. The problem is exacerbated by the rush to implement new learning technologies based on the promises of lower costs coupled with dramatic productivity gains without a real foundation in place. The promises are real, but in many cases unrealized. Organizations need a strong foundation. We can do better; we must do better.

Learning must outpace change for organizations to survive and individuals to thrive.

These are the most exciting times ever to be involved in learning and helping individuals and organizations to grow their intellectual capital. Learning is a vital component of success in our knowledge economy. Learning must outpace change for organizations to survive and individuals to thrive. New technologies enable us to do things never before possible. But we mustn't allow technology to guide our strategies. We must begin with performance and learning, then build our strategies and use technology to appropriately implement the strategies. Only then can we realize our potential.

■ A Hierarchical Framework

The key to success is to focus on learning, not technology. We hear so much today about communications and computing technologies that it is easy to begin with neat technology and to forget that learning is the ultimate goal. Taking a hierarchical approach helps to ensure that your ultimate implementation tactics and technologies will meet the business and performance goals of your organization.

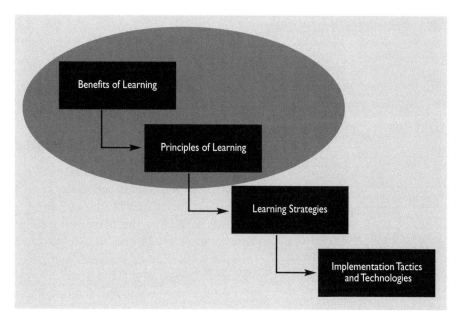

This hierarchy begins with some fundamental beliefs and principles about learning. These beliefs and principles ensure a solid foundation for learning. The learning strategies, implementation tactics and technologies put the principles into action and allow you to build effective learning solutions. The beliefs and principles remain constant regardless of the technologies available. As new technologies emerge, these beliefs and principles allow you to make informed decisions about how to alter your strategies, tactics and technologies to take advantage of new technologies as appropriate. The key to success is getting the first two components of the hierarchy right.

■ *Beliefs on Learning*

Technology changes rapidly. It's hard to develop a cohesive long-term learning strategy if you begin with technology. What doesn't change is the foundation of what makes learning work. Building a learning strategy that starts with these basic beliefs provides your learning strategy with a solid foundation. Every learning strategy should consider the following basic beliefs.

➤ Learning must enhance **performance** — individual and organizational.

➤ Learning is an ongoing **process**, not a single event.

➤ Learning must be **learner-centered**.

➤ Learning must be **engaging** — the experience matters!

➤ Learning must be **targeted** — the right learning, at the right time, for the right people.

➤ Learning must be **integrated** to accelerate performance.

➤ Learning must be linked with **knowledge management** to optimize performance.

➤ Your learning strategy must be **appropriate** to your needs and resources.

■ *Principles for Learning: Some Best Practices*

Each of these basic beliefs can be expanded to principles for learning. These principles serve as best practices for implementing a learning strategy.

➤ **Performance:** *Learning must be linked to performance — individual and organizational*

Some people may make the case that any learning is inherently good. In an altruistic world that may be true, but adults learn best when they understand the relationship between learning and their own personal motivations. Learning must have clear links to the learner's job and/or his or her own personal and professional goals. That means that learning must be designed in a way that it is clearly relevant to what the learner needs to be successful. If not, it is difficult at best to capture and maintain the learners' attention. The design should also be flexible enough to address specific learner needs. If one learner needs more background, detail or practice to be able to perform successfully, then the learning design should allow for that learner to obtain the additional information. Likewise, if a learner is "catching on" quickly, they should be able to proceed through the learning more quickly. Finally the learning should be timed to happen as closely as possible to the performance need. When learners clearly see the pending need for new skills or knowledge there is a "teachable moment" when they are more open to learning.

➤ **Learning:** *Learning is an ongoing process, not a single event*

The very nature of training and traditional classroom instruction led to an "event" based mentality about learning. Training was scheduled, everybody had coffee and donuts, and at the end of the event you were trained. In reality, learning is an ongoing process. It is facilitated by trial and error and experimentation as critical components of the learning process. By including assessment and feedback as part of the process, learning can be adaptive to match the level of progress and proficiency of individual learners. Segmenting learning into appropriate chunks supports this adaptive learning process. Because learning is a process, tracking and measurement systems are an important part of managing the learning process. We know from research that only 30 percent of learning happens through structured learning events. Learning should be designed as part of a process and positioned to be readily applicable to real life

Learning should be designed as part of a process and positioned to be readily applicable to real life situations.

situations. The other 70 percent of learning happens on the job. Treating learning as a process, it can be designed in a variety of ways that support that on-the-job learning process. Short chunks of e-learning available on the fly, electronic performance support systems, knowledge tools and access to knowledge management systems, and collaboration tools can and should be appropriately applied to support the unstructured, on-the-job learning process. By using these multiple strategies and activities, learning is reinforced over time.

➤ **Learner-Centered:** *Learning must be learner-centered — content needs to be compelling*

Traditional training experiences were, almost by definition, centered on the instructor of the course material. The learner took a secondary role. The learner must become central to the process. Effective learning must tap into individual learner's motivations. The content that is delivered must meet a compelling need of the learner to achieve task performance. It should be designed to closely resemble the specific work or task requirements. The learning should also be designed flexibly to meet individual learner's needs so that they can learn when they are ready to learn, meeting their specific challenges on their schedule at their pace, and when and where it is convenient for them.

➤ **Engaging:** *Learning must be engaging*

It's not enough for the design to be learner-centered and compelling; it also needs to be interactive and dynamic. The design should accommodate or match a learner's preferred learning style. And although the learning should take place in a risk-free environment, learners need to be held accountable for learning and performance; there needs to be learning tension. Finally, the learning should be a rewarding experience. It should not only be enjoyable, but learners should readily see the benefits to them in helping them to perform more effectively.

➤ Targeted: *Learning must be targeted — the right learning, at the right time, for the right people*

One of the easiest ways to get the attention of learners is to effectively target the learning; it should be tailored to fit the audience. "One size fits all" just does not work effectively. Learning is also most successful when targeted at skills that are important to performance. But, be selective when targeting learning. Skills and competencies can be innate or developed through training and experience. Some skills are more easily developed than others are and learning should be targeted at skills and competencies that lend themselves to development.

➤ Integrated: *Learning must be integrated to accelerate performance*

Learning can't be seen as something separate from the job. It needs to be designed and positioned as an integral part of the job, not an additional activity. Performance support tools and job aids are effective methods of integrating learning as part of real-time job performance. Effectively combining learning, performance support tools and job aids can minimize the time needed for structured learning events and shorten time required to improved performance.

➤ Knowledge Management: *Learning must be linked with knowledge management to optimize performance*

Learning by itself is just not enough to drive performance. An important component of learning is the ability to locate and access appropriate information and the intellectual capital of others. Learners need access to and understanding of relevant information to successfully drive performance. Because information is hierarchical and relative, it should be accessed and viewed based on the learners' needs, perspective and experience.

➤ Appropriate: *Your learning strategy must be appropriate to your needs and resources*

Finally, your learning solution must be appropriate. There are many different options available when choosing a learning strategy. Your strategy should be tailored to meet your organizational performance and timing requirements. Ultimately, the learning strategy should fit with your organizational culture — or take into account needed cultural changes required as part of the implementation. When developing the learning strategy it's critical to consider current and planned technology infrastructure. In the end, your learning strategy must also take into account resource commitment and constraints.

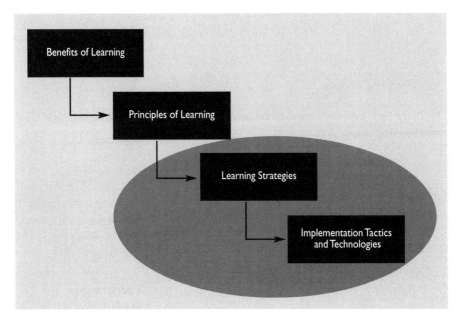

■ *The Rest of the Framework*

These basic beliefs and principles provide the foundation necessary for an effective learning strategy. Many of these beliefs are reminiscent of a time when learning was an individual one on one activity that occurred between an apprentice and master. To some extent they have been lost during the industrial age. Effectively applying technologies as part of an integrated learning strategy allows organizations to get back to the basics. We've only begun to scratch the surface of what is possible. Each of the principles raises important implications for how you should develop your learning strategy, implementation tactics and the technologies you will use. Ultimately, your choices will come back to what is most appropriate for your organization. But remember, no matter what you do, always begin with business strategies and performance needs.

Chapter 5

Getting Started in E-learning and Ensuring a Successful Finish

By Barry Howard

■ *The E-learning Crush Has Arrived*

You know that e-learning is here. You see it at every turn, every conference, and every HR event. You have probably experimented with some tools already. You have an enthusiasm, a curiosity, a concern or worse, an objective for 2001. So you read this chapter and hope that it will provide a quick solution to the e-learning startup process. Sorry. If I were selling something, I would say that the quick solution is just around the corner. If I were really a consultant, I would say that the magical matrix, flow diagrams and checklist that you can give to a subordinate would do it all. Having spent many years as the Director for NYNEX and Bell Atlantic's Distance Learning programs, spoken at too many training conferences and sat with too many corporate managers just like you, I can insist

. . . the magic isn't in the technology or the quick fix, it is really in the same strategic approach you use for every major business culture change.

that the magic isn't in the technology or the quick fix, it is really in the same strategic approach you use for every major business culture change. In fact, that may be a magic key to get the process started, but not the successful finish that you really want. But, I'm getting ahead of myself.

■ *Everyone Is Getting Started*

If you are reading this feeling alone and isolated, forget it! Most of the organizations I have worked with are all "just getting started," even those who have transitioned a significant number of courses to some form of e-learning. In some ways, too many organizations have gone through many e-learning trials and pilots, only to wind up wondering when the real, promised values will occur. Worse yet, organizations with a highly fragmented HR structure (by department, by business unit, etc.) have as many trials running as they have HR organizations. The result is a proliferation of tools, protocols and plans that never come to fruition. Lots of getting started, rarely a "getting finished."

■ *Grabbing the Change —What an Opportunity*

Every organization is in the process of change. Some are more public than others. Some have a program for every year (Mergers, Acquisitions, Quality, Process Engineering, ISO9000, etc). These change processes absorb all of the organization's uncommitted funds, frequently reducing other budgets like HR and training. Fight the current monster? No! Use its momentum to power your e-learning effort by inserting your program inside their plan. Because most of these changes have major impact on line functions, and because the real payoff of e-learning is in the line, the smart HRIM manager will find a way to link the two early in the new project cycle. The sell will be particularly easy when the geography is diverse. Training is a part of the change, and the PC has found its way to most desks and homes.

■ *Barry Howard's Mistakes*

Identifying the change process to align with your e-learning plan is the easy part. Selling the concept, as indicated above, will also be easy. The hard part is the actual approach taken by the champion of the change, YOU. The alternatives include the pilot approach (tactical), or a series of pilots, leading to a comprehensive plan and the strategic approach. Want to take the easy, safe approach, start with the pilot. Everyone else seems to be doing it and that is what I did at NYNEX.

I started with a pilot in computer-based training (CBT). From there it was multimedia, then CBT creation, learning centers, videoconferencing adapted for learning, group-based, network-supported learning (now called the virtual classroom), video LANS, electronic performance support systems and finally network- delivered, self-paced training. Spread over 10 years, the plan seemed sound. Each trial could be carefully constructed and carefully executed with a strong evaluation plan. Risk was reduced by selecting simple applications to friendly users. The successful pilot could be turned into a production tool. The ones that didn't pan out could be put back on the shelf for the future, or discarded as lacking value. When completed, one of every three courses to existing employees was being delivered through some electronic media.

Sound good to you? It sounded good to me, but it had a number of flaws. Because it lacked an overall, comprehensive plan, many of the efforts conflicted. The conflict was in courses, markets or resources.

Because it was not integrated in other HR systems, it stood by itself and grew only when the trainers made it grow (not the students or their managers). Because the e-learning was in a separate organization, it did not impact the enormous initial training for new employees that was being accomplished by the traditional, separate training organizations.

"We had built it, but they only came when asked." I have learned that there is a better way, especially now many years later, with the value of e-learning accepted by virtually all large organizations.

■ *Don't Do It Like Barry — Use the Strategic Approach*

The strategic approach still uses the mechanism of the pilot. The pilot, however, is implemented under the direction of an overall, comprehensive plan that ensures that all of the key change elements are satisfied up front. In addition, the strategic plan creates an expectation within management, that the organization itself will pass through four major stages,[1] and that each change element will appear different for each stage.

Creating this long-term plan is tedious and takes time. It means lining up support before the pilots can prove anything. It exposes your strategy before the first results come in and exposes that strategy to the leaders of your organization because of its impact. It exposes your knowledge of best practices and of the technologies themselves and it leaves a chance for someone to say no.

Aligning the plan with the major change in your organization, mentioned previously, can increase the chance for a yes.

■ *What are the characteristics — Key Elements*

The major change elements include the following. They are by no means complete, but demonstrate the many facets of the change element process. If you think the list is long, just visualize FOUR TIMES THE AMOUNT. See the next section about that.

Compensation	What special ways will e-learning be rewarded to stimulate interest and completions?
Customer Impact	Will the e-learning be used to reach the organization's customers in addition to the internal staff?
Design	What special arrangements have been made for the unique design requirements of e-learning?
Funding — Chargeback	How will the e-learning be paid for? Will there be a chargeback?
Geographic Impact	How will the e-learning plan be implemented? Which area first? How much will be covered?
Implementation	How will the implementation be done? By department, by geography, by job title, by level?
Integration in HR	How will the e-learning plan fit within other e-HR programs like assessment, appraisal, career development, succession planning?
IT Infrastructure	What changes will be required in the IT infrastructure to make the e-learning work?
IT Involvement	When and how will IT be involved in the planning effort?
Learner Impact/Culture	How will the e-learning affect the environment of the learner?
Linkage — Not HR	How will the e-learning plan be integrated in the budget, staffing, security and other non-HR organizational functions and systems?
Location Strategy	Wheere will e-learning be taken? At the desk, in the building, at home, at a hotel, etc.
Management Engagement	How will managers be a part of the e-learning introduction and operation?
Motivation	How will learners be motivated to start taking the e-learning courses?
Objectives	What internal objectives will be changed to accomodate the new e-learning?
Organization	How will the training organization be changed to deliver the e-learning?

Performance Management	What performance management indicators will be used to measure the effectiveness of the e-learning?
Promotion	What publicity efforts are planned?
Stakeholders	Who are the key players? Who cares about what is happening to your plan? Who is actively championing your case?
Support Systems	At what stage are the support systems (registration, evaluation, career development) being devoted to e-learning?
Tools Used	How many e-learning tools are in play? Whic ones are they? Are self-paced, group paced, electronic support systems being used?
Tracking/Measurement	How is the e-learning being measured? Are non-traditional tools being explored? Are you capturing the one-minute lessons, the non-business time for learning moments?
Training Competencies	What new skills has your team developed? Course authoring, vendor management, project management, curriculum integration, web synch delivery, e-mail learning, etc.
Vendor Strategy	Are you using in-house or outsourced resources? Are you seeking many independent vendors or a few tactical ones?

■ Looking at the Steps is Not Enough — Plan the Phases

I realize it is a long list, however, unless you mention each of the items on the list your business plan will be incomplete and your chances for failure increase. The other complication is the way that you create expectations for each of them, for example:

Stakeholders	Who are the key players? Who cares about what is happening to your plan? Who is actively championing your case?

In your business plan, you might indicate that everyone in the organization would be engaged in the e-learning process. Imagine the senior manager HR who funds your vision and allows you to get the first pilots started, only to find his/her peers return a "ho-hum" when your e-learning is brought up. How much better it would be if you had described the changes as multistage. Zane Berge, in his soon-to-be published *Sustaining Distance Training*[2] describes four stages of technology-delivered learning.

➤ **Stage 1: Sporadic Courses.** Separate or sporadic distance learning events occur in the organization.

➤ **Stage 2: Continuous Operation.** The organization's technological capability and infrastructure can support distance learning events. When distance education events occur, they are replicated through an interdisciplinary team that responds to staff and management needs and makes recommendations regarding the organization and management of distance learning among the workforce.

➤ **Stage 3: Policy Developed.** The organization has established a distance learning policy, procedures are in place and planning occurs. This means that a stable and predictable process is in place to facilitate the identification and selection of content and of technology to deliver distance training.

➤ **Stage 4: Integrated Everywhere.** Sustainable Distance training and education has been institutionalized in the organization as characterized by policy, communication, and practice that are aligned so that business objectives are being addressed. The business unit has established a distance education identity and conducts systematic assessment of distance training events from an organizational perspective.

Now, let's look at that stakeholder issue. If we anticipate that our organization will also go through the four stages, perhaps the senior executive would have seen the same chart expanded to show:

Stakeholders	Who are the key players? Who cares about what is happening to your plan? Who is actively championing your case?
Stage One: Only those associated with the pilot will be aware. The line manager's selected for their interest in e-learning will be actively involoved and will want credit for their "out-of-the-box" thinking.	
Stage Two: Senior department managers, shown the results of the pilot, will now be clamoring for more e-learning on a wider geographic, departmental or subject matter scope.	
Stage Three: Managers who are associated with change processes (IT, finance, Communications, etc.) will now be a part of the process, demanding the benefits be spread over even larger constituencies.	
Stage Four: All Senior managers will assume e-learning is a part of the HR repertoire, expecting that it will be considered before other delivery methods.	

■ Using the Project Plan as a Planning Tool

One of the best tools to get the process started is project management. By identifying key milestone dates, key responsible players, list of tasks and sub-tasks, relationships between activities, parallel and serial tasks, etc. senior managers can get a visual view of the plan, where each stage will fall and when resources will be needed. I recommend that the training manager use a simple tool (e.g. Microsoft Project) to create Gantt, CPM and other documentation to support the plan. With all four stages developed and added to the timeline, the senior manager will have less concerns in approving the "getting started, Stage One" plan, knowing the ultimate impact that it will have.

> *The training manager should focus on the benefits to the line organizations before looking for the savings to the HR department.*

Of course, spread sheets to document return on investment (ROI) are also needed, documenting the major areas of saving. The training manager should focus on the benefits to the line organizations before looking for the savings to the HR department. The former can easily be 10 times the latter and far more important to the overall organization.

The business plan itself will probably fit into a word document including many of the following sections:

➤ Objective,

➤ Executive Summary,

➤ Current Situation and Issues,

➤ Alternatives,

➤ Recommended Action,

➤ Key Obstacles,

➤ Benefits,

➤ Next Steps, and

➤ Summary.

■ Getting the Job Done — Resources

With the project plan in hand and the approval document signed, it is time to find the right people to get the job done. There is work to be done, and even when heavily outsourced, must have direction and supervision from your team. I have heard clients say they want help in getting started, then back away from all responsibility. Here are some examples of the tasks:

Task	Potential Resources
Writing the business plan	Line manager, training director
Design the pilots	Training developer, technologist
Selecting the courses	Focus groups, senior manager interviews
Selecting the tools	Training developers
Writing the RFI's, RFP's	Consultants, purchasing department
ROI calculations	Consultants, financial managers
Implementing pilots	IT, delivery team
Evaluating the pilots	Automated data gathering, voice mail systems, interviews by outsiders
Project management	Key Department champion
Communications planning	PR staff with training delivery team
Culture changes	Line manager, focus group or steering committee, outside assistance
Integration with other HR programs	HR specialist, IT, consultants

■ You Are Not Alone

With e-learning growing at its current rate, you don't have to work the issues on your own. Lots of helpers are around and many will work for free in exchange for good networking. Here is a partial list:

Helper	Comments
Other departments within the organizaation	Get a senior manager involved to insure cooperation, not competition.
Other similar organizations	Use your industry association to identify these. Avoid direct competitors, though, for obvious reasons.
Other organizations	Get out to the HR and training conferences like IHRIM, SHRM, ASTD, Training 2001, ISPI, etc., or those only focused at e-learning like Tech Learn, On Line Learning, etc.
Vendors	Just remember what their motivation is.
E-Learning Consultants	Should be unbiased, but need to understand the practical issues of your organization.
Academic Institutions	Your local college may be smart enough to provide some partnerships that will benefit both of you.
Publications	E-Learning is the subject. Try the online publications first. They use the medium and are more up to date (watch out for commercials).

■ Getting Started Right Will Mean Getting Finished

I hope that by this time in your reading you will stop the impulsive pilot after pilot strategy and build an e-learning plan that demonstrates what you are starting today will deliver the benefits that you have promised tomorrow. And even if tomorrow is in four or five years, you will still be following the plan to get you there. Add the helpers, add the tools, add the vendors and then your students and the rest could be another best practice. And if I have added something to your planning thoughts, then let me know.

■ Endnotes

1 Zane Berge, *Sustaining Distance Educaton*, (Jossey Bass, November 2000).

2 Jossey Bass publisher, 11/2000 first Edition, follows the award-winning "Distance Training."

Chapter 6

Learner Success in Distance Education Environments:
A Shared Responsibility

By Howard Major and Nancy Levenburg

Student success has become a primary focus of today's educational institutions and is an area of national concern. The successful mastery of academic content, once viewed entirely as the learners' responsibility, is now considered a shared responsibility between three major players: the student, the instructor, and the educational institution.

Literary tracts on successful strategies for traditional classroom environments are legion. Less understood and written about are strategies for effective learning in distance education environments. Learning in distance education environments requires unique strategies that may be initiated by the instructor, the institution, and/or the learners themselves. The purpose of this chapter is to describe these strategies. First, though, we need to consider the characteristics of distance education.

■ *What is Distance Education?*

Distance education occurs whenever the instructor and the learners are not in the same location at the same time. Figure 1 illustrates that the instructor and learners may vary with regard to their spatial and temporal locations. If they are in the same place at the same time (upper left quadrant),

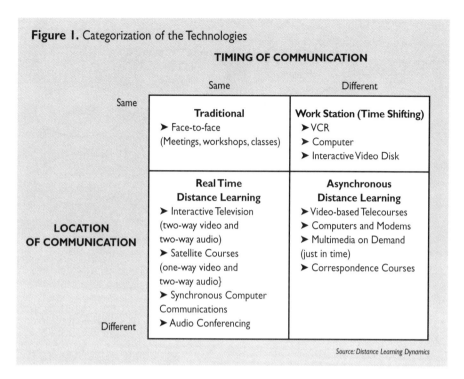

Figure 1. Categorization of the Technologies

then this is not a form of distance learning. The other three quadrants depict situations in which the instructor and the learners are either in different locations (lower left quadrant), or operating in a different timeframe (upper right quadrant), or both (lower right quadrant). While the term "distance education" implies that the location-shifting capability is of paramount importance, many times learners are more interested in the time-shifting capabilities provided by technology-based distance education systems than they are in the location-shifting capabilities of the systems. For this reason, some educators use the term "virtual education" rather than "distance education" to describe these systems.

■ The Role of Educational Technologies in Distance Education

Distance education systems must deploy educational technologies capable of surmounting the barriers of time and location. Formerly, print-based correspondence courses led the way. Today, distance education is moving toward a

Figure 2.

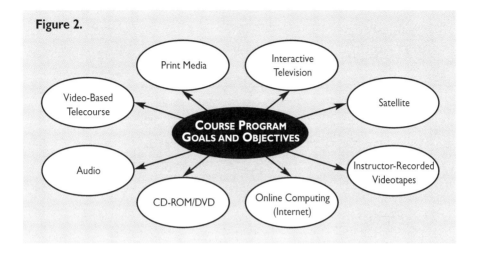

"blended" technology approach deploying multiple technologies (Major and Levenburg, 1997).

Figure 2 depicts graphically that learning outcomes (goals and objectives) should be at the center of the decision-making process, and that communication technologies should be selected based on their ability to facilitate established desired outcomes.

Using the metaphor of a "toolkit," educators select and apply the appropriate distance education "tool" to facilitate students' engagement in optimally appropriate learning activities for the outcome being addressed. In the Major-Levenburg Distance Learning Curriculum Matrix (Figure 3), the instructor begins at the top center with the pre-instructional analysis and then proceeds clockwise to make the critical distance education instructional design decisions. The pre-instructional analysis provides baseline information about the learners and their entry-level skills and aptitudes as well as information about available toolkit resources. The next steps are: (a) the establishment of appropriate learning outcomes for those learners in that learning environment; (b) the development of assessment strategies to assure that, after the measurement of learning outcomes, there will be measured, suitable modifications to facilitate the learners' achievement; (c) the selection of the most appropriate learning activities; and (d) the selection and deployment of the best technological tool(s) for supporting those learning activities. These steps ensure precise reasons for the selection of particular technologies in each instructional instance. The learning environment may call for the use of several instructional technologies, just as a home-repair situation may require the carpenter to use a variety of tools from her/his carpentry "toolkit." But for too long, the application of educational technologies has been described best by the adage, "When all you have is a hammer, everything looks like a nail."

Figure 3.

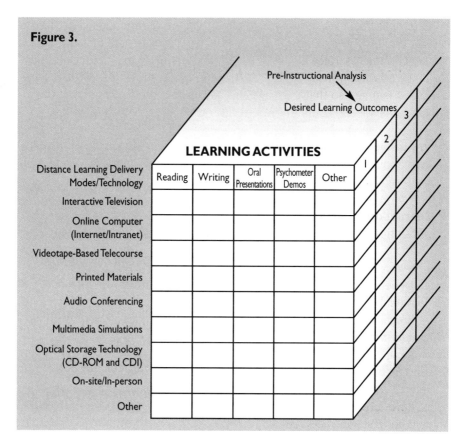

In emerging distance education systems, the entire educational technology toolkit is available to instructors and to learners; this implies an obligation for the institution to provide access to the entire range of educational technologies and for instructors to learn how to use them effectively.

■ Distance Learning Success Strategies Initiated by the Instructor

As the instructional leader, the instructor typically plans the instructional outcomes, selects much of the content of the instruction, and ascertains how successful learning will be achieved, measured, and assessed. The instructor sets norms for interaction and controls the pacing and communication patterns of the learning environment.

In a traditional classroom teaching and learning situation, much of this occurs at the unspoken, almost subconscious level. However, in distance education environments, roles are less defined; the instructor must articulate them. Distance education instructors must provide many structures for themselves and their learners so that everyone will have a clear understanding of the expected behavior and communication patterns:

➤ **Pre-instructional analysis.** Conduct a pre-instructional analysis for information about the learners, available resources, and technology tools, and the barriers and constraints to overcome or circumvent.

➤ **Learner orientation.** Provide learners with a thorough orientation to reduce uncertainties, provide clear guidelines for success, clarify expected performance and behavior patterns, and establish the direction of the learning experience. Depending on the communication tools available to the instructor, this orientation can take the form of a live session held in an interactive television environment, a videocassette prepared by the instructor and mailed to learners, or an introductory online session. Students who have completed the orientation should understand what is expected of a successful learner in the instructional environment; they should also know how to access specific technological tools and feel comfortable using them.

. . . specifically identify the behaviors the successful learner will be able to perform upon completion of the learning experience.

➤ **Course outcomes.** Clarify expected course outcomes, which should specifically identify the behaviors the successful learner will be able to perform upon completion of the learning experience. These outcomes are often listed as course goals and objectives.

➤ **Instructional design.** Apply established principles of instructional design, including: (a) conducting a pre-instructional analysis of the learners' characteristics and goals and the resources and barriers in the learning environment; (b) identifying desired learning outcomes; (c) selecting and deploying learning activities and technologies that best lend themselves to learner achievement of course outcomes; and (d) determining methods of authentic learner assessment in achieving specified course outcomes.

➤ **Practice and feedback.** Provide learners with opportunities to practice learned behaviors and receive corrective feedback with regard to their performances.

➤ **Authentic assessment.** Apply principles of authentic assessment in diagnostic, formative, and summative contexts. In other words, measure learners' entry levels as they relate to course objectives, check for progress along the way, and measure their achievement of the objectives with criterion-referenced measurement instruments at the end of the instructional process.

➤ **Communication protocol.** Establish appropriate communication patterns and guidelines, model desired communication patterns, demonstrate use of distance education technologies for communication and interaction, and reward assertive and constructive learner communications.

➤ **Constructivist learning.** Model learning processes that are effective in distance learning environments; be one learner in a community of learners; move from the mental model of "teacher as a dispenser of learning" to one wherein the instructor is a facilitator of a shared constructivist learning process.

➤ **Technology selection and deployment.** Apply the appropriate instructional tool(s) to the instructional process to optimize learning.

➤ **Print materials and graphics.** Distribute printed materials in advance and convert graphics and other display materials to appropriate formats for the distance learning technologies being employed. Graphics and other materials that cannot be clearly seen will kill an otherwise effective instructional process.

■ Distance Learning Strategies Employed by the Institution

The institution that accepts the responsibility of delivering education at a distance must also make certain structural and systemic changes to support the emerging learning environments. For example, technical assistance must be available at all times. This probably means assigning technicians to the second and third shifts, so that someone is available around the clock. Other learner and instructor support strategies include:

➤ Extending library services to students at "remote" locations. Some institutions have established an "outreach librarian" position to support off-campus learners and instructors.

➤ Making counseling and other student services personnel available to learners in remote locations and those who participate in learning at unconventional times.

➤ Making academic advising available to distant and/or time-shifted learners.

➤ Committing the institution to establishing a total technology toolkit so that instructors are able to select appropriate technological tools for helping learners achieve a specific outcome.

➤ Investing in substantial professional development for instructional personnel. Instructors, counselors, administrators, librarians, and other educators must have access to professional development opportunities in order to apply the technology toolkit effectively (Major and Levenburg, 1997). To address a poor track record in this regard, Richard Varne (1996) advocates that 25 percent of distance education budgets be set aside for professional development. In reality, closer to three percent is allocated nationally, which often results in instructors being unable to use available technology.

In rewarding the use of emerging technologies, institutions must implement compensation systems, using either release time or financial compensation. Planning distance education delivery is a time-consuming process. Some institutions reward this with compensation during the time period when the planning takes place (the semester before delivery of the course or training activity), rather than waiting until the instruction is actually delivered. Intangible rewards and recognition systems may also encourage distance education planning and delivery. In addition, institutions should make a point of employing instructors who are the products of distance education delivery; educators who will have a visceral understanding of the process. This will model an appropriate regard for the effectiveness of distance learning per se; it will also eliminate the current ethical dilemma that exists when institutions offer distance education programs but discriminate, in their employment practices, against the products of distance education programs.

. . . institutions should make a point of employing instructors who are the products of distance education delivery; educators who will have a visceral understanding of the process.

To provide optimal flexibility in packaging and access, distance learning delivery should design combination modules of courses and/or entire degree or certificate programs. In other instances, learners may desire single modules applicable to their performance at their place of employment. Modularization is a step toward the "just-in-time performance enhancement" systems predicted by Perelman (1992).

Institutions should encourage a distance education delivery "team-planning" approach, consisting of an instructional designer, a librarian, a continuing education representative, technicians from appropriate technical areas, and, of course, the instructor. This planning team will help secure needed resources; it will also assure that the various components work cooperatively. Some institutions are experimenting with a new team-teaching approach: two or more instructors play different "roles" in the course delivery. For example, instructors with excellent lecture styles may videotape their lectures. Others that excel in analyzing learner writing and providing insightful feedback may monitor online class discussions. This role differentiation allows instructors to operate more effectively.

■ *Distance Learning Strategies Employed by the Learner*

It is the learner's responsibility to be an active learner; passivity is typically not rewarded in distance learning environments. Learners can contribute to their own learning success by:

➤ **Self-directed learning.** Two behaviors that characterize the self-directed learner in distance learning environments are self-discipline and meta-cognitive processes. Since learners may choose when they will actively engage in the learning process (time-shifted learning), they must have the self-discipline and time-management skills to "keep up" with the expected learning schedule and pace. Learners must accept the importance of this demand, or opt out of the distance education environment. Since employers expect similar skills, distance education should tout this expectation as an advantage rather than apologizing for it.

The second required behavior, the meta-cognitive process, entails the learners asking themselves if learning has taken place. If the answer is "no," the learners must either repeat the previously engaged-in learning activities or ask for help. This process differs from many traditional learning systems in that in some distance learning environments, instructors cannot read non-verbal cues to detect learners in trouble. Again, as meta-cognition is a valuable lifelong skill, educators should not apologize for requiring it.

➤ **Using technology.** Distance learners must learn to use specified communication technologies. This involves problem-solving and pro-active approaches to acquiring instructors' help.

➤ **Working together.** Distance learners should help other learners and work together, and thus become less dependent on the instructor. Students often find that the learning they create communally is far richer than that gained from a single presenter. The instructor becomes a community member and functions with his students to create the learning rather than simply dispensing it. Dialogues then occur among learners and between learners, and the instructor no longer adheres to a traditional top-down academic hierarchy in which the knowledge flows one way from the instructor to the learners (Jonassen, 1995).

■ *Conclusion*

Several groups must share responsibility for successful learning. While this is true in all learning situations, it is particularly important in distance learning environments. Without shared responsibility among instructors, institutions, and learners, distance learning systems will function poorly and break down. Distance education environments require the articulation of the mental model presented here so that administrators, instructors, and learners understand and can fulfill their roles.

Source: Howard Major and Nancy Levenburg. "Learner Success in Distance Education Environments: A Shared Responsibility." Technology Source, *January 19999. Reprinted with permission of the authors.*

■ References:

Jonassen, D., M. Davidson, M. Collins, J. Campbell, and B. Haag, (1995). "Constructivism and Computer-mediated Communication in Distance Education." *The American Journal of Distance Education.* (9), 1995, pp. 17-23.

Major, H. T. and N.M. Levenburg, "Critical Issues in Interactive Television Delivery: Instructional Quality, Faculty Development and Faculty Compensation." ED 413 867 (ERIC Document) 1997, p. 14.

Major, H. T., and N.M. Levenburg, "Designing Multiple-Technology Marketing Courses. *Marketing Educator*, 1997, p. 8.

Perelman, L. J., *School's Out.* New York: Avon Books, 1992.

Varne, Richard. Keynote address, National Telelearning Conference, Chicago, IL, 1996. The Telecourse People and The Instructional Telecommunications Council of the American Association of Community Colleges.

Chapter 7
E-Lessons Learned

By Kathy Carrier

This chapter provides practical, real-world tips related to e-learning. We have experienced the joys and frustrations of this growing delivery method of learning. Summary points in the following areas will be covered:

➤ Cost-justifying the project

➤ Benefits of e-learning

➤ Objectives and outlines

➤ Content gathering and approval

➤ Learner testing

➤ Budget and timeline

➤ Our typical process

➤ Marketing and promotion

➤ Pilots, data tracking and continuous improvement

■ Cost-Justifying the Project

The investment a company makes in the creation of e-learning is significant, as compared to traditional training. The development of e-learning programs can be as much as three to five times the cost of the development of classroom training. The reasons for this are related to the "glitz" and the programming effort. The identification of visuals, graphics and sound adds additional cost. Also, the cost to tie the written and visual pieces together through programming is significant. Typically, we pay 30-50 percent more for programming talent than we do for an instructional designer. This is especially true if the program is built from scratch rather than using canned software programs.

Following is a simple matrix that can be used to cost-justify e-learning. We find that most programs can be cost-justified if you review the payback over a three-year period. Thus, this matrix should be completed for both a one and a three-year period.

Annual Cost Variables	Option #1 Classroom Instruction w/Workbook	Option #2 CBT with Limited Content	Option #3 Complete CBT Solution
Instructional Design Cost			
Trainer Salary/Benefits			
Programming Fees			
Trainee Efficiency			
Printing Costs			
Content Revision			
Total			

Employee turnover can be a major selling point. Many companies struggle with high turnover and the continual need to train employees. E-learning is a way to provide consistent, high quality training to new employees.

E-lesson learned: Most projects can be cost-justified if you review the cost/benefit over a multi-year period.

■ Benefits of E-learning

Following are some of the benefits that we highlight as we promote our e-learning capability:

➤ **Consistency** — consistency of training content and delivery

➤ **Test Scoring** — opportunity to collect and aggregate scoring data

➤ **Floor Space** — limits the need for training rooms because existing employees will learn at their desks

➤ **Fewer Trainers** — reduces the need for trainers, focuses trainer attention on development

➤ **Morale** — builds morale and enthusiasm for the company and work area

➤ **High-Tech Image** — presents a positive, high-tech image to new employees

➤ **Scheduling** — simplifies scheduling and delivery of training for existing staff

While e-learning may cost somewhat more than traditional classroom instruction, the benefits are substantial and can easily be cost-justified over three years.

➤ **Transfers** — assists in training employees who transfer into the unit

➤ **Interactive** — inherently interactive and oriented to all four adult learning styles

➤ **Trainer Turnover** — provides consistent program in the event of trainer turnover

➤ **Generation X** — more attuned to younger employees, a large percent of the new employees

➤ **Geographically Dispersed Learners** — learners who are geographically dispersed can access the learning through the intranet or Internet

➤ **Mastery of Knowledge** — assures participants master content through periodic testing

➤ **Efficient Use of Time** — trainees proceed at their own pace

➤ **Existing Employees** — provides online learning tool at no additional cost for existing employees who lack knowledge

➤ **Future Investment** — reduces the cost of future CBT programs: the opener, interface and other components can be used in future CBT programs

■ *Objectives and Outlines*

We develop several types of objectives. The first objectives that we develop relate to the broad objectives of the training program. What does the company hope to accomplish through the implementation of the program? The second set of objectives relate to the learner. What should the learner be able to demonstrate and know following the program? We have found that it is critical to write, discuss, and get these approved before proceeding. Otherwise, you will spend needless time and money on the revision of the instructional design and programming.

Once the objectives are set in stone, the course outline should be developed. This is the framework for the e-learning. One good way to incur needless writing and programming cost is to change the outline or framework in the middle of the project.

E-lesson learned: Cast the objectives and outline in stone early in the project.

■ *Content Gathering and Approval*

Gathering accurate and complete content can be a monumental bottleneck. It is essential that you have all interested parties cooperate in gathering good, solid content at the start. Otherwise, you will experience huge delays. Accuracy of the content is also essential. Some client-assigned content gatherers have given us outdated information or inaccurate information. Once programmed, you won't want to change it and incur the additional cost. So determine who your content gatherer is, and keep him/her on schedule.

Content approval can be a headache as well. Occasionally, the training department will be in a turf war with the marketing and communications department over course ownership. This leads to different people with different perspectives all wanting to see a different version of the content. My advice is to stay out of the politics and work through one person who manages the egos. With the significant investment for e-learning and the fact that it is popular and new, we find that many of the client officers want to approve the e-learning. These officers often don't agree.

Find one person that handles the approval process and funnel all the executives through that person. With one client, we went so far as to require them to sign an approval page for each module. This can be a huge bottleneck, as well as a politically touchy situation. It can also increase the cost of the project for the client and decrease your profit.

E-lesson learned: Require that the client gather and approve the content for you and hold them to the established timetable.

■ Learner Testing

The ability to test the learner online, record the data and requeue the learning is an advantage over typical classroom training. The adult learners we work with aren't as threatened by online reviews and quizzes as compared to tests administered in a classroom. Beware! Your company in their performance management process may use this data. We had one client who was interested in using the data to determine who should be let go. If you plan to do this, you need to make sure the test is legally validated and will stand if challenged in court. Another thing to know is that collecting and tracking the results can be a costly programming issue.

E-lesson learned: Online quizzes and testing are useful. However, complex tracking of test results can be costly to the program.

■ *Budget and Timeline*

Good luck sticking to your budget and project timetable. We have found that revision, reorganization, staffing changes and direction changes frequently. These changes can cause significant delays and can dramatically hinder your ability to complete the project on time and under budget. It is more difficult to change the course of the training with e-learning than it is in the traditional classroom world.

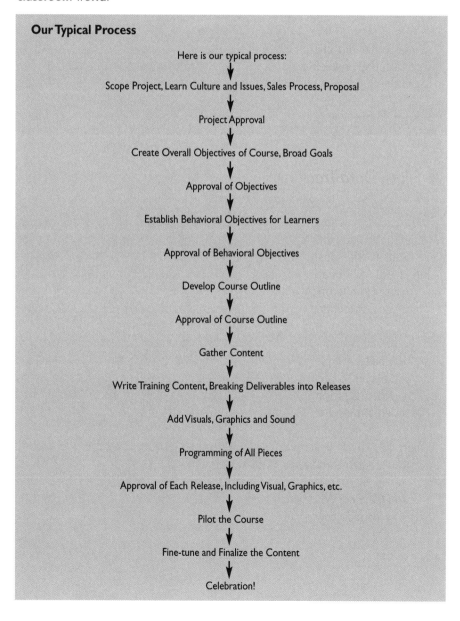

Our Typical Process

Here is our typical process:
↓
Scope Project, Learn Culture and Issues, Sales Process, Proposal
↓
Project Approval
↓
Create Overall Objectives of Course, Broad Goals
↓
Approval of Objectives
↓
Establish Behavioral Objectives for Learners
↓
Approval of Behavioral Objectives
↓
Develop Course Outline
↓
Approval of Course Outline
↓
Gather Content
↓
Write Training Content, Breaking Deliverables into Releases
↓
Add Visuals, Graphics and Sound
↓
Programming of All Pieces
↓
Approval of Each Release, Including Visual, Graphics, etc.
↓
Pilot the Course
↓
Fine-tune and Finalize the Content
↓
Celebration!

E-lesson learned: Build unforeseen delays into the timetable and unpredictable cost to the budget.

■ Market and Promote the Project

We find that our clients are quite interested in e-learning projects. At the end of each day or week, we post the most current version to our website. This enables clients to view progress of the project on a daily basis.

■ Pilots, Data Tracking and Continuous Improvement

We've learned to pilot the e-learning in the real world. We do this midway through the project, and at the end as a fine-tuning process. This provides practical input to the design process. "Live" programs don't always go as we planned. This will enable you to do two things: predict timing accurately and ensure maximum learners' retention.

Once your project is complete, you will want to focus on tracking the data and continuous improvement. Tracking the user data can be cost prohibitive. One of our clients defined tracking so complex that it would take two programmers eight months to complete the programming. We shared this with our client, and when she began to breathe again, she chose to be realistic and track only the employee identification numbers.

Also, recommend to your company that they budget for continuous improvement and added modules. One of our large clients budgeted for updating the data to reflect a predictable level of change in their company. Also, the budget included for added modules of learning.

E-lesson learned: What you will create will become outdated, so have the client budget for periodic content revision.

■ *Feeding Frenzy*

Last year, we were approached by several venture capitalist firms to merge our company with various technology firms. The goal, of course, would be to create an e-learning powerhouse. We completed the due diligence process and I spent six solid weeks putting the investment deal together. I created and revised countless balance sheets and pro-forma financial statements. It was very time consuming, especially the time that I spent coaching my nervous employees through my thinking. During the six-week process, many other suitable technology partners emerged. There seemed to be very few firms that understood adult learning and training, but a plethora of technology firms with the "ultimate software solution." No one had a sales and marketing capability. Of course, that would have been my responsibility. I eventually chose to merge with none of the companies and to keep the venture capitalists out of our lives.

E-lesson learned: Beware, e-learning technology firms are everywhere. Good, sound adult instructional design firms are not.

E-learning Blueprints

Chapter 8

Designing Online and In-Person Education and Training:
The Same Difference?

By Zane Berge, Ph.D.

For many years, I have been known to say that I teach in-person and online "the same way." Do I really? Should instructional design for online instruction be any different than that for in-person instruction? For purposes here, online instruction is defined as instruction in which the graded portion of the course is significantly computer-mediated or Web-based. Why would the teaching methods used or the activities assigned to learners be changed simply because the delivery system used is different? Should materials development, course implementation, student evaluation, or the course evaluation itself be done differently when we are teaching an online course versus an in-person course? For effective learning to take place, must the management of the online class-room be done differently compared to an in-person class?

■ *What Is Good Instruction?*

In general, I would not place many of the traditional, on-campus courses on a pedestal as shining examples to emulate online! Much of the traditional in-person teaching follows an industrial model that is as outdated in today's Information Age as buggy whips were to modern transportation soon after the turn of the 19th century. Using this antiquated model for teaching and learning would mean we're preparing learners for a world long since gone (Berge, 1999), a world in which educators could teach learners in four to six years, for the most part, all they needed for their life-time of work in a particular field. Today, it is realized that educators do not have a chance of such an outcome. For the last several decades in education, there has been a shift from an instructor-centered approach to a learner-centered approach. To be effective, good instructions begin by acknowledging that the world in which the learner lives is one of multiple careers and characterized by changing disciplines.

■ Structuring Instruction

A way to view one goal of the instructor or designer is to plan the instructional activities for the student at a level that is neither too little, too late, too early or too much! In the ideal, it would be creating a learning environment that is perfect in structure for each individual learner. Further, it can be thought of as the instructor working him or herself out of a job i.e., the instructor's ultimate goal is to develop autonomous learners. To accomplish this, online instructors and designers must know their learners and design instruction to the learners' level.

With novice learners ...

there is a need for more

instructor-centered

approaches,

even direct instruction

at times.

Each learner desires structure in novel learning situations. When I say learners need or demand structure, what I mean is they demand that the instructor supplies the structure, rather than the learners supplying it for themselves. With novice learners, regardless of age, there is a need for more instructor-centered approaches, even direct instruction at times.

> The strategies used for constructing course designs must increasingly account for learner-determined and learner-navigated paths while also continuing to established instructor-directed and domain-dependent learning parameters, as appropriate (Wagner, 1998, p. 7).

Still, the overall goals and the course expectations in learner-centered classrooms is for the direction to be away from instructor-directed activities and toward student, self-directed learning. Thus, "exceptional instructors recognize the importance of balance between what is provided for the student and what the student should independently and responsibly seek" (Johnson, 1989, p. 64). It is clear that employers need employees who are self-directed learners, and a continuously learning workforce to compete in today's global marketplace (Berge, 2000; Schreiber and Berge, 1998).

■ Quality of Instruction

Instructional design determines quality. Or, at least, it puts a ceiling on how effective the course or program can be. Certainly, poor materials development, poor delivery, or a dozen other variables can cause a course to be less effective than it was designed to be. According to the World Bank:

> There is almost universal agreement that the effectiveness of distance learning is linked more closely to the quality of instructional design and learner support than it is to the technology used. Thus educators can increase effectiveness by ensuring that course design, student support, and instructional strategies reflect an understanding of the key factors in student satisfaction, achievement, and persistence.

Of course, that is true of in-person courses as well as online courses. Quality in education and training starts by matching the instructional goals and objectives with authentic, real-world problems or projects. It continues by aligning the content, the practice students engage in, and the evaluation with those objectives that have been determined for the course. It is by following these design principles that the instructor or designer sets the limits on the effectiveness (i.e., quality) of the instruction.

■ Factors Affecting Learner Satisfaction, Achievement and Persistence

On a philosophical level, online or in-person instruction is the same. But, when we move to the actual course level design, development, implementation, evaluation, and support, there are significant differences as we will see below. This chapter focuses on design and evaluation as examples of these differences.

Four areas that are important in affecting satisfaction, achievement and persistence are:

➤ learner-centered approaches

➤ design elements

➤ evaluation

➤ learner support

There are dozens of factors within these areas that deserve to be explored. Given space limitations, only a few will be briefly addressed below to give you a sense of the scope and at what level design differences occur between in-person and online education and training.

■ Learner-Centered Approaches

Learner-centered approaches go a long way in allowing learners to share in setting and achieving high standards. Learner-centered does not mean laisse-faire. It does not mean that there is no structure imposed by the instructor. If that were true, the learning would be more in the realm of self-study. While these approaches are not new, what is new is the widespread shift in emphasis throughout education and training, and the emergence over the past two decades of technology systems capable of allowing learning environments to be created that are easier, faster, and more convenient than in the past. Of course, a challenge for designers is accounting for the learner-determined and learner-navigated paths to learning and at the same time balancing instructor-directed and domain-dependent learning parameters as is needed (Wagner, 1998).

■ Selected Design Elements

Regardless of anything else, design must lead to clear instructional goals. Learners must know what is expected of them. It should be said several times, that planning for online activities and learning must be done sooner and more carefully — with more detail — than is generally necessary for the in-person classroom.

In general, any instruction goal or objective can be met in an online environment. However, it is critical to remember that the pacing is different — it usually takes considerably more time online to accomplish the same goals, especially if those outcomes have to do with such methods as working in teams or developing skills in which learners analyze, synthesize or evaluate.

In the space here, let's take a look at a few other elements important to note differences in the design of online and in-person instruction:

➤ Interaction/Structuring Learning

➤ Collaboration

➤ Media Selection

➤ Motivation

➤ **Interaction/Structuring Learning.** Learning seems to occur in stages or according to a pattern. In knowledge acquisition, learners are exposed to concepts and ideas that are presented to them by someone else — a textbook author or the instructor. At some point, mental models begin to form in each individual student, and that student begins to seek answers to internal questions and hypotheses. The student is not (only) acquiring hand-me-down knowledge, but is also aware that knowledge is useful and can be managed to satisfy one's own constructs about the world and how it works. Understanding is broadened by reasoning, argumentation and problem solving as learners become more autonomous and constructive in their learning process. Finally, learning shifts to self-evaluation and self-reflection, not only on the knowledge products and problems solved, but also on the processes and strategies that were effective (Hartley and Collins-Brown, 1999).

In knowledge acquisition, learners are exposed to concepts and ideas that are presented to them by someone else — a textbook author or the instructor.

In an instructor-centered, in-person classroom, strategies along these lines can take place quickly and readily. Feedback from learners to the instructor, both explicit and through non-verbal cues, help the instructor adjust the level and methods to better meet the needs of the class participants. In an online environment, student levels of knowledge acquisition versus higher-order learning must be anticipated to a much greater degree than in the typical in-person classroom. Again, planning for the successful online classroom needs to be done sooner rather than later.

➤ **Collaboration.** There has probably been more written about collaboration and teamwork in the business management and educational classroom literature than just about anything else. Collaboration here refers to learning that demands learners work together by dividing the tasks or performances, helping each other, and offering each other praise and criticism appropriately (Gage & Berliner, 1992). This collaboration needs to not only produce the desired products, but do so in a harmonious way among the participants. The outcome for each individual's learning is planned to be more than that individual could obtain if not working collaboratively.

... the size of teams matters when working online in a classroom environment. While four to six may be an ideal group size in-person, half of that should be considered online — and add in a lot more time.

It has been my experience that, although we require collaboration and partnerships in both school and the workplace, neither student nor professor, nor employee or manager, really know what teamwork is, how it can be made successful, why it sometimes fails, or what to do to prevent or repair damage to a team. I encourage everyone to have persons who will be involved collaboratively to learn about it first. Secondly, I have found that the size of teams matters when working online in a classroom environment. While four to six may be an ideal group size in-person, half of that should be considered online — and add in a lot more time.

➤ **Media Selection.** I mentioned the need to consider adjusting team size for online classes. Class size may also be a factor when going online:

> " . . . the size of a distant class can affect the selection, use, and effectiveness of technology in facilitating teaching and learning. A class for hundreds is quite different from a class of 15. In the former, certain technologies, such as video- or audioconferences, might be more effective than IRC or e-mail (Zhang, 1998).

Plan the interactions learners will experience — interactions between learner and instructor, learner with content, and learner among their peers.

Think about whether each interaction should be self-paced and asynchronous, or occur in real-time. Such decisions about media mix are not new. Instructors have been using lecture, demonstration, discussion, video/film, textbooks, and other delivery channels for centuries. What is somewhat new is the ease of use of good quality, two-way communication channels offered by the Web and other computer-mediated communication systems. The challenge for instructors and designers is to use each medium to the best potential in the service of teaching and learning.

➤ **Motivation.** Without the daily or weekly face-to-face contact and opportunity for in-person feedback that contact allows, learners sometimes have trouble self-evaluating their progress. Designers of online instruction need to provide opportunities for feedback from learners to the instructor and vice versa, whenever possible. Otherwise, the lack of these opportunities (even if these opportunities are not taken by learners when provided) often has a significant affect on student motivation and hence lessens the dropout rate or the persistence that learners show online.

■ *Evaluation*

Evaluation can occur on many levels. For instance, we can evaluate the student's learning, student's perceptions, the course's overall effectiveness or the program's efficiency and effectiveness and how the course contributed to that. While evaluation can be done the same for online courses and in-person courses when it comes to an individual learning, the instructional evaluator must remember that there is a technology component that is overlaid in this system. It may affect learner achievement, but it will almost certainly affect learner satisfaction with the course.

Modifying evaluation instruments to include special requirements of distance education or specific delivery systems is useful. The modifications to evaluation of online teaching are through questions about participation online, familiarity with the various aspects of the required technology, student involvement in online activities such as discussion groups, and the degree of student involvement in moderated or unmoderated online seminars. Thus, student perceptions of these issues help designers to improve future programs, and helps decision-makers to judge the overall value of programs.

■ *Learner Support*

Solid learner support includes logistical support (IDE, 1997). Examples of this include, making sure all learners are treated equally when it comes to having materials available to them to complete assignments. If written exams are chosen by the instructor, access to proctored exam sites need to be arranged, with whatever level of security is deemed appropriate. If learners incur expenses such as long-distance phone charges, a system needs to be in place that states clearly the policies and procedures for reimbursements.

Learner support needs to be changed to accommodate distance learners in the systems developed for in-person learners such as academic advising, registration, and housing. How instructor availability and access to library materials will be handled must be made clear to learners at a distance. In-person learning often relies on resources such as science laboratories or computer software and hardware. The instructional goals need to either be met with alternative assignments, or the resources deemed necessary need to be made easily accessible for learners at a distance, (e.g., lab kits; interactive video network systems; videotaped experiments; computer simulations; learners traveling to a location with the necessary production facilities occasionally).

■ *Conclusions*

What I mean by teaching the same online and offline, is that I have held a learner-centered philosophy since before going online, and before the shift in the past few decades away from the instructor-centered approaches in the classroom. Therefore, unlike many of my colleagues, I did not need to change roles to as great an extent while simultaneously learning to use technology in the service of teaching and learning. But closer reflection of the planning, implementing, evaluating and managing of an online versus in-person classroom makes it clear that, at this different level, I do several important things differently regarding design, evaluation and learner support.

What really matters? Is it that the philosophy one holds that is the same regardless of whether the instruction is online or off? Or, is it the details in the design, development, implementation, evaluation, and management of the course — dozens of factors that do change depending upon the learning environment and communication channels that are used? Whether online or off, a course must meet the needs of learners' satisfaction, achievement, and persistence. It all matters.

■ References

Berge, Z.L. (Ed.), *Sustaining Distance Training: Integrating Learning Technologies into the Fabric of the Enterprise.* San Francisco, CA: Jossey-Bass, 2000.

Berge, Z.L., "Educational Technology in Post-Industrial Society." J.G. Webster (Ed.) Wiley *Encyclopedia of Electrical and Electronics Engineering* Volume 6. NY: John Wiley & Sons, Inc., Publishers. 1999, pp. 187-197.

Gage, N.L. and D.C. Berliner, *Educational Psychology* (5th ed.). Boston, MA: Houghton Mifflin, 1992.

Hartley, J.R. (Moderator) and E. Collins-Brown, (Summarizer), "Effective Pedagogies for Managing Collaborative Learning in Online Learning Environments." *Educational Technology & Society* 2(2) [Online.] [Accessed on 8/30/00.] http://ifets.gmd.de/periodical/vol_2_99/formal_discussion_0399.html

IDE (Institute for Distance Education). "Models of Distance Education." [Online.] [Accessed 8/2/00.] http://www.umuc.edu/ide/modlmenu.html.

Johnson, K.A., "Instructional Design and the New Teaching Technologies." *Instructional design: New alternatives for effective education and training.* K.A. Johnson & L.J. Foa (Eds.), pp.: 63-71. New York: Macmillan Publishing Company, 1989.

Schreiber, D.A. & Z.L. Berge, Z.L. (Eds.), *Distance Training: How Innovative Organizations are Using Technology to Maximize Learning and Meet Business Objectives.* San Francisco, CA: Jossey-Bass Inc., Publishers, 1998.

Wagner, E.D., "Designing Courses for Distance Education." Presentation at the Distance Education Workshop: Partnerships to Stay competitive in a Networked World. University Continuing Education Association. Chicago. April 3, 1998.

World Bank. Global Distance Educationet. [Online.] [Accessed 8/2/00.] www.globaldistancelearning.com/Management/Benefits/effectiveness.html

Zhang, P., "A Case Study on Technology Use in Distance Learning," *Journal of Research on Computing in Education,* 30 (4), 1998, pp. 398-420.

Chapter 9
Web-based Learning:
Extending the Paradigm

By Dirk Rodenburg

Although Web-based learning has been touted as a panacea for many training and educational needs, the reality is that results can fall dramatically short of expectations. Unfortunately, dominant conceptions of Web-based instruction for many organizations are primarily driven or shaped by IT personnel and departments, not by educators. In my work, servicing a primarily corporate clientele, this is often the case.

Those issues that are educational in nature — such as sustainable content management, sound pedagogical strategy, and learner support — are all too often left in the periphery. I'd like to discuss some ways in which the discussion around learning technology can be broadened to include a more critical, more effective approach to design and implementation.

■ *The Challenge: Using the Technology Appropriately*

Education is a complicated construct. The vast range of competing perspectives offers many different, legitimate ways of characterizing process and outcomes (Pratt, 1998). The problem for the designers of a technology-based learning strategy is defining an instructional paradigm that is contextually appropriate and instructionally sound from this myriad of conceptual frameworks.

In my experience, many Web-based learning environments do not reflect a coherent and carefully considered instructional approach. More often than not,
the developers of technology-based learning environments make the following
assumptions, which are not supported by research:

➤ Learning efficacy is related to the amount and visual richness of the media
provided

➤ Access to information is the same as instruction

➤ Simple "ad-hoc" assessment is usually a reliable indicator of learning outcomes

■ *Media and Learning*

Research into the impact of media on learning outcomes does not support
an unequivocal endorsement of a "technology" or "media-centric" approach
(Clark, 1985, 1987). I've found that many technology learning initiatives support
an uncritical acceptance of the following relationship:

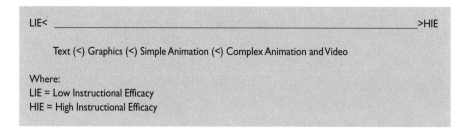

LIE< _____ >HIE

Text (<) Graphics (<) Simple Animation (<) Complex Animation and Video

Where:
LIE = Low Instructional Efficacy
HIE = High Instructional Efficacy

The value of novelty, which is often used as a rationale for the inclusion of
more band-width intensive media — "We've got to get them excited!" — is not
sufficient to provide sustained instructional efficacy. What does contribute to
instructional efficacy is the contextual appropriateness of the media used and
the ways in which the learners engage with that media, in terms of the stated
learning objectives.

■ Contextual Appropriateness of Media

Contextual appropriateness within a Web-based learning environment is related to a number of issues, some of which include:

➤ *What level of representation is appropriate for the learning objectives?* In some cases, a simple conceptual diagram will suffice. In others, dynamic representations of process flow or variable interaction are important. In others, a narrative or story coupled with specific imagery is crucial to help learners understand the impact of macro forces at the micro level, or to foster personal engagement with the issues under discussion.

➤ *How can the media utilized be provided in a manner that fosters, not hinders, the learning experience?* This issue is in part technical and in part design-related. If download or access times are prohibitive, learners will experience frustration. If the media is abstracted too much from the context in which it is meant to be supportive (i.e. downloaded and viewed later, or launched through a separate proprietary set of applications), learners will lose the connection between context and media element.

➤ *How can the media utilized be effectively presented?* This is also an issue that is both technical and design-related. For example, in many contexts, a "layered" delivery of an image or diagram (through channels like "FLASH(tm)" or DHTML) is a bandwidth conservative method for representing changes in structure resulting from changes to a single variable or a combination of variables.

■ Learner Interaction with Media

The ways in which the learner will engage with the supporting media is a second important consideration with two associated issues:

1. To what extent can the learner control the presentation of the media to match his/her needs? Let's look at a simple example, online video. In my experience, many Web-based learning approaches assume that inclusion of a supporting video resource is sufficient to provide effective instructional support. Depending on context, that can be true. But the use of online video can often be augmented to provide more effective, better-targeted instructional support. For example, an online video resource can be segmented into topics or concepts or can be linked to keywords (or meta tags) and instructional/curricular goals. In this way, direct, nonlinear access to specific segments of interest can be provided to support or help resolve conceptual difficulties.

2. How can media be structured to allow the learner to interact with and/or self-discover underlying principles, models, and causal relationships? Using online video as an example again, a specific event can be shown from a number of different perspectives (cultural, sociological, economic, age, role, disability, and so on), or as a consequence of a specific conceptual model ("What happens to the ball in a vacuum when it is no longer pushed? What about the same situation in normal atmosphere?"). By providing a method by which each (competing) perspective can easily be comparatively viewed, or each predicted outcome tested, learners can begin to formulate, articulate and test new conceptual frameworks.

■ *Instruction and Access to Information*

Providing access to information is not the same as teaching, but this distinction is often blurred by developers of Web-based learning programs. In fact, simply providing access to information can, in some cases, do more damage than good. Learners can experience anger, resentment and frustration if mechanisms for distribution, access, and learning do not meet expectations.

Constructing meaningful representations of knowledge takes time, commitment, and an appropriate level of organizational/institutional support. Design goals should include helping the learner to:

➤ Understand, reiterate, consolidate, and review the overall constructs of the learning material

➤ Identify and articulate existing knowledge, models, and constructs concerning the learning material being presented

➤ Examine and evaluate the coherence, predictive validity, and completeness of existing knowledge and models

➤ Understand the relationship between a specific construct and the overall constructs of the learning material

➤ Identify, examine, and evaluate competing ways of understanding the learning material

➤ Discriminate between material essential for understanding those constructs and material presented as adjunctive explanations or resources

...Web technology offers the added dimension of the ability to respond dynamically to learner choice.

Many of these techniques are currently used within the context of print (e.g. textbooks), but Web technology offers the added dimension of the ability to respond dynamically to learner choice.

For example, few Web-based learning applications attempt to provide consistent, easily-accessed, and well-structured ways in which the following questions can be answered:

1. What are the overall objectives of the material I'm now covering?

2. How does the information I'm reviewing now fit into those overall objectives?

3. What have I covered so far?

4. What do I still have to cover?

5. How am I thinking about this material?

6. How do other learners typically think about this material, and how well do those ways of thinking map to my own?

7. What are some of the consequences of each way of thinking about the material?

8. What are some of the typical misconceptions that learners have as they study this material?

9. What are better ways of thinking about this material that are tied to those misconceptions?

10. How is what I'm learning now going to help me deal with later material?

11. What's essential for me to pay attention to right now, and what's important for later?

■ *Assessment: A Tool for Instruction and Measurement*

Web-based learning approaches often use a paradigm that completely separates learning material and assessment. The typical learner experience is to "cover" a specific learning module and then immediately complete a short assessment process (usually multiple choice) that tests for immediate recall of the information. The learner is then free to return to the module or move on to the next based on performance within the assessment. This vision of assessment has some serious instructional shortcomings (Elstein, 1994, Ramsden, 1993, Page, 1995, White and Gunstone, 1992).

A more integrated approach would be to include assessment within the instructional process. For example, after a new concept has been presented, learners could predict the consequences of a range of variables applied to a theoretical model, or pick a way of thinking about the problem domain that best matches their own, or both. The feedback generated by these choices could provide some insight into (and therefore the potential for developing a diagnostic framework for) the way in which the learner is conceptualizing the material. These "instructional assessments" within the instructional material can help the learner articulate the way in which he/she is thinking about the problem (meta-cognition) and understand the predictive value or short comings of that approach, as well as the degree to which it generally accounts for the problem domain.

> *Wrong answers should not be treated as wrong answers ("there are never stupid questions, only stupid answers").*

One way to develop this kind of "embedded" feedback is to involve teachers who have experience teaching the specific topic under consideration. Content expertise is one thing; pedagogical expertise within a specific domain space is another (Pratt, 1998). Teachers can help identify specific points at which learners typically encounter difficulty, and, equally importantly, describe misconceptions that are often carried by learners. The instructional material and assessment and feedback mechanisms can then be designed to anticipate common needs.

Wrong answers should not be treated as wrong answers ("there are never stupid questions, only stupid answers"). They are pointers that show how the learner conceptualizes the instructional material and that can help designers plan targeted instructional support.

■ Objectives for Online Design

Online learning design should do more than provide access to information; it should support the following processes:

➤ Extracting and articulating existing conceptual frameworks and prior knowledge

➤ Testing the predictive and explanatory value of these frameworks within the domain space under consideration

➤ Orienting and focusing on the relationship between new information and concepts and existing frameworks

➤ Testing the predictive and explanatory value of these reworked frameworks within the domain space under consideration

➤ Integrating new concepts into elegant, holistic and meaningful representations

---

Source: Dirk Rodenburg, "Web-based Learning: Extending the Paradigm," Technology Source, November/December 1999. Reprinted with permission of the author.

■ References

Clark, R. E., Evidence for Confounding in Computer-Based Instruction Studies: Analyzing the Meta-Analyses. *Educational Communication and Technology*, 1985b, 33(4), pp. 249-262.

Clark, R. E., "Which technology for What Purpose? The State of the Argument About Research on Learning from Media." Paper presented at the annual conference of the Association for Educational Communications and Technology, Atlanta, GA, 1987.

Elstein, A. S., "What Goes Around Comes Around: Return of the Hypothetico-Deductive Strategy. *Teaching & Learning in Medicine*, 1994, 6(2), pp. 121-123.

Page, G., "Developing Key-Feature Problems and Examinations to Assess Clinical Decision-Making Skills," *Academic Medicine*, 1995, 70(3), 194-201.

Pratt, D. & Associates, *Five Perspectives on Teaching in Adult and Higher Education*. FL: Krieger Publishing, 1998.

Ramsden, Paul, "Theories of Learning and Teaching and the Practice of Excellence in Higher Education," *Higher Education Research and Development*, 1993, 12(1), 87-97.

White, R. and Gunstone, R., *Probing Understanding*. London: The Falmer Press, 1992.

Chapter 10
The Guiding Assumptions of Successful Distance Education Programs

By Barry Willis

In a few short years, distance education and its off-spring (e.g., Web-supported instruction, video conferencing, etc.) have been transformed from a quaint irrelevancy to a lightening rod for change on many university campuses.

Sherron and Boettcher (1997) suggest that the current rush to implement distance learning programs by colleges and universities is occurring for three major reasons:

➤ The convergence of communication and computing technologies,

➤ The need for Information Age workers to acquire new skills without interrupting their working lives for extended periods of time, and

➤ The need to reduce the cost of education.

These reasons and others have attracted hopeful politicians and others with minimal background and little previous interest to distance education. Others who view distance education as the "Trojan Horse" signaling "the commodification of higher education" have been equally moved by distance education for quite different reasons (see Noble, 1997, 1998, 1999). It is ironic that the politicians who trumpet the benefits of distance education the loudest know relatively little about it, while those who see a dark side to the use of educational technology feel quite comfortable using the Web and related media to espouse their views. Irony aside, the accompanying claims of what distance education can and can't, should and shouldn't do have resulted in an ever-widening gap between the rhetoric and reality of distance education. Closing this gap can be accelerated by thoughtfully considering what could be labeled "Distance Education's Best Kept Secrets:"

■ 1. Distance education is about increasing access, not making money.

Those who look to distance education as a revenue-generating machine resulting in financial windfalls for their programs or departments are typically disappointed when they factor in the true costs of this endeavor (see Oppenheimer, 1997). These costs include hardware/software, system maintenance/upgrading, telecommunication/transmission charges, technical support, faculty/program development and evaluation, student support, and myriad personnel and infrastructure costs associated with these vital components and services. The importance of these critical and continuing costs and constant technological change usually necessitate the reinvestment of virtually all income generated by the enterprise. Those who take profits typically do so at the expense of needed upgrades with the potential risk of losing whatever market share they fought to win in the first place.

This is not to say that distance education is without its financial benefits. Many Land Grant institutions, for example, provide statewide educational programs and services. A few years ago, this could entail chartering aircraft to fly faculty to remote outreach or extension centers in various locations served by the Land Grant Institution. Even today, it is not unusual for faculty to drive 200-300 miles a week to meet with students located far from campus. The costs of such enterprises in terms of time, energy, and faculty goodwill are excessive.

In contrast, the appropriate use of distance education can be cost effective, even if the end result isn't a financial windfall. What does result from the appropriate use of technology may be even more beneficial: the ability to maintain and even grow the market for institutional programs and services. Given the rural and cloistered nature of many of our best Land Grant institutions, the ability to reach out to students wherever they reside is a huge competitive advantage and a potential determining factor in enhancing or even maintaining institutional viability.

■ 2. There is no technological "silver bullet" — not even the Web.

Every new technology is accompanied by its share of advocates proclaiming it to be the ultimate delivery tool promising to solve all instructional problems, even those that are yet to be fully understood. In reality, a poorly defined problem has an infinite number of solutions, we just never know which one is the most appropriate. Until instructional needs are understood in detail, any technology could be appropriate...or inappropriate.

Even those at the forefront of technological innovation, including Bill Gates of Microsoft and Andrew Grove of Intel, candidly admit they are unsure where the future of technology will lead their companies (Grove, 1999). As a result, they invest heavily in marketing, research, and development in efforts to maintain their technological preeminence wherever the future might lead them.

For institutions without the research and development funding to invest in every potentially beneficial instructional delivery innovation, the best advice is to avoid technological solutions in search of instructional problems. Instead, focus on the requirements of the content to be delivered, the needs of the learners being served, tangible instructional opportunities (e.g., the need to train a computer-literate cadre of highly-motivated professionals), and potential obstacles (e.g., limited bandwidth to the locations you serve). Attend to these requirements and the most appropriate technological solutions will make themselves apparent. In this context, the primary benefit of the Web is not as a delivery system in and of itself, but as a standardized platform from which various technological solutions can be launched.

Nevertheless, those who think the Web is the ultimate solution to all instructional problems should review the research literature of the 50s stating the same thing — about the overhead projector.

■ 3. The only constant in the world of instructional technology is change.

Anticipating change and technological directions is always challenging and filled with uncertainty. Move too fast and your technological upgrade will be obsolete before it is fully implemented. Move too slowly and your programmatic market share could slip before you can catch up. Just as damaging, failure to innovate will signal your competition and potential markets that your program is no longer viable.

In a world of technological change, timing is everything. Those who learn to embrace technological innovation when the timing is right will be the big winners. The rest will be left to fight over the crumbs.

■ 4. Lasting technological change is typically the result of evolution rather than revolution.

Over the past 30 years, technological innovation has evolved in a fairly consistent manner. This process could be referred to as technological birth, death, and resurrection. In the "birth" stage, new technologies emerge, unrealistic expectations are set, and the potential impact of the new tool is over-hyped. In the "death" stage, the original outspoken advocates move on to the next innovation, general enthusiasm gradually fades, and interest wanes as the realities of what the new technology can and can't do emerge. Finally, in the "resurrection" stage, thoughtful reflection occurs as the new technology is tested in various, often random, instructional settings. While the technological innovation is found inadequate in most applications, it proves beneficial in addressing a limited number of specific needs.

Over time, the once-proclaimed technological cure-all takes its place among other teaching tools and fades from the forefront of technological innovation — into the hands of those who can put the benefits of the technology to best use.

It is for this reason that few effective instructional experiences are anchored to a specific technology. More often than not, a variety of technologies, each filling a specific and well-defined role, are woven together by a skilled educator into instructionally sound and technologically transparent academic experiences.

■ 5. The emphasis of distance education should be in the quality of the academic program, not in the use of technology.

Selecting technology is easy compared to the focused attention and subtle insights needed to design, develop, and implement a truly effective academic program. This is why the skilled teacher will continue to play the preeminent role in successful academic encounters, regardless of the sophisticated technology being used.

Similarly, instructional delivery experiences that rely almost solely on technology (e.g., first generation Web-based courses) with little apparent influence and day-to-day involvement by a thoughtful and skilled teacher, may generate initial student interest. Without adequate course design, there may be little lasting enthusiasm for the overall instructional program, or the motivation to complete the course that originally offered so much promise.

The best that can be said about the management of technology is that someone has to do it... and do it right.

Finally, successful program administrators will spend adequate time and resources to nurture and support those creative and concerned faculty who are willing to take the leap of faith required to be successful in the distance education enterprise.

■ 6. There is no glory in managing instructional technology.

You'd think there would be, but there isn't. Keeping up with technology is a never ending battle filled with unmet expectations, too few resources, and the need to constantly plan ahead realizing that the technology that you are implementing today is likely already dated and on the road to obsolescence.

The best that can be said about the management of technology is that someone has to do it...and do it right. Without exceptional management skills and a thick skin, the implementation of technology is an impossible task that gives those involved the illusion that they are in control, when in reality they are at the mercy of technological innovations that don't exist today, but will be demanded tomorrow.

■ 7. Learning is enhanced when technology is used to directly link students to other students.

The lack of effective and personalized student-student interaction and feedback is the potential "Achilles heel" of distance education. Conversely, the need for effective distant student-student interaction provides a great opportunity to creatively use technology. In fact, whether it is teacher-to-student or student-to-student interaction, learning is enhanced when technology is used to improve communication (see Flottemesch, 1999).

In my experience, effective instruction almost always requires that a fully-engaged teacher establish the learning framework, even when the target audience consists of highly motivated adults. Also of critical importance is the learning that takes place when students are linked to other students...without any teacher present. Given the inherent separation that is evident in most distant learning environments, it is difficult for many students to maintain any continuing connection to the instructional context, let alone the content being presented in any given course. By creating learning spaces and technological linkages that bring distant students together as groups and as individuals, the gaps between what is being taught and what is being learned can often be bridged (see Wallace & Weiner, 1998).

■ 8. Face-to-face instruction is still a valid delivery method in support of distance-delivered courses — when possible.

The ideal scenario is to bring students from all sites together for an intensive day or two early in the course and incorporate group process techniques to foster cohesion and unity of purpose among participants. Ending the semester with another intensive face-to-face session at which time final projects are presented and course objectives are summarized is a beneficial capstone experience. If time and budget permit, meeting an additional time or two during the semester will likely prove both academically useful and personally rewarding.

Undoubtedly, incorporating "real time" interaction increases the logistical challenges of any distant course and requires faculty and student sacrifices as they struggle to match schedules. In some cases, however, the sacrifices are worthwhile and often essential. In the case of technical courses, for example, where laboratory experiences are critical to successful course completion, the question isn't "if" face-to-face communication can be incorporated, but "how" it will be accomplished. The challenge is then to maximize the time of faculty, facilitators and students, while scheduling the technical facilities needed to accomplish it.

Despite the potential benefits derived by focused personal contact, many educators (and even more administrators) feel that incorporating face-to-face communication in distant courses is expensive and defeats the inherent flexibility and perceived lower costs that initially attracted them to distance education.

Depending on where the course is being delivered, it may be physically impossible to bring the teacher and students together. Nevertheless, it is better to rule out personal contact as impractical or instructionally irrelevant than it is to fail considering it in the first place. When the logistics can be successfully navigated, teachers and students alike are rewarded by well-planned and highly interactive face-to-face contact.

■ 9. Many faculty are comfortable when distant students from other institutions take their classes, but don't like their students taking classes from faculty at other institutions.

This is a major stumbling block to cooperative distance education ventures and has limited the success of strategic partnerships relying on the sharing of faculty expertise. The best partnerships are forged when specific academic needs are identified and on-campus expertise is absent. In these cases, competition is not a factor and both sending and receiving institutions benefit. Despite being a major institutional and political motivator for the initial start-up of distance education efforts, true academic alliances have proven elusive and are the exception, not the rule.

Until the culture of course "ownership" moderates and the "not invented here" syndrome fades, wide-scale institutional cooperation will be more a goal than a reality.

■ 10. At its core, distance education is a change process, not a delivery system.

Historically, higher education culture has proven resistant to change. Perhaps the greatest benefit of distance education is its potential role as a catalyst for change in the way educational institutions do business. In a relatively short span of years, the proliferation of programs and services available at a distance have resulted in a heightened sense of competitiveness unheard of in higher education. For institutions that are up to the challenge, the current interest and growth in distance learning presents a new opportunity. While the dangers of competing and failing in this new world of educational access may pose significant problems, the refusal to aggressively move forward may be the greatest risk of all.

By any standard, distance education has proven to be a useful tool for educators and administrators who have taken the time to adequately assess its strengths and weaknesses. Continued success will require the careful planning, implementation, and tracking of distance education successes and failures.

This discussion keeps leading back to one incontrovertible conclusion: Distance education is one piece of the educational delivery puzzle, but not the "answer" to all program delivery challenges facing educators today.

There is little doubt that distance education has the potential to positively impact higher education. The greatest gains will only occur, however, after the opportunities and limitations of technology-supported delivery are critically reviewed and realistically analyzed. The sooner this happens, the better — for teachers, administrators, and most of all, the students who stand to gain the most through innovative solutions to the myriad delivery issues educators and society face today.

■ References

Flottemesch, K., "Building Effective Interaction in Distance Education." *Educational Technology Journal*, (In Press), 1999.

Grove, Andrew, Charlie Rose Television Interview, Program #2407, Bloomberg Television. New York City, NY, 1999.

Noble, D.L., *Digital Diploma Mills, Part 1: The Automation of Higher Education*, 1997, http://communication.ucsd.edu/dl/ddm1.html.

Noble, D.L., *Digital Diploma Mills, Part 2: The Coming Battle Over Online Instruction*, 1998, http://communication.ucsd.edu/dl/ddm2.html.

Noble, D.L., *Digital Diploma Mills, Part 4: Rehearsal for the Revolution*, 1999, http:// communication.ucsd.edu/dl/ddm4/html.

Openheimer, T., "The Computer Delusion," *The Atlantic Monthly*, 280 (1), 1997, pp. 45-62. http://www.theatlantic.com/issues/97jul/computer.htm.

Sherron, G.T. & J.V. Boettcher, J.V., "Distance Learning: The Shift to Interactivity. *CAUSE Professional Paper Series*, #17, Boulder, CO, 1997.

Wallace, D.R. & S.T. Weinter, S.T., "How Might Classroom Time be Used Given WWW-Based Lectures? *Journal of Engineering Education*, 87 (3), 1998, pp. 237-248.

Chapter 11

Identifying Promising Innovation Initiatives in Workplace Learning and Technology:
Three Logs Might Burn, Four Logs Will Burn

By John T. Thompson and Tom T. Carey

■ Introduction

Continuous and dramatic innovation in the area of Internet-based technology, and growing acceptance by managers that knowledge is an important organizational resource are stimulating a tremendous amount of innovation in the realm of workplace teaching and learning. New models of education and training are being developed, new software being created, new practices developed and introduced. Innovation and experimentation are in the air. There is a sense that the old rules no longer apply. Thus, knowledge management writers often present their ideas as new, as revolutionary, and as a solution to the problem of not reinventing the wheel. But for observers steeped in the history of educational reform, it seems that there is a lot of reinventing the wheel going on in this new economy.

The introduction of innovation into teaching and learning situations is not new. Innovation and reform has been a prominent and recurring feature of school-based learning for decades. But the history of school reform is predominantly the history of the failure of school reform (Elmore, 1996; Sarason, 1982). If one accepts Santayana's dictum that those who forget the past are doomed to repeat it, it seems reasonable to expect that many of the teaching and learning innovations (e.g., knowledge management) now being introduced into workplace settings will suffer a similar fate. After significant investments of time and attention and money, many, if not most, of these innovations are going to fizzle out. They are not going to catch fire.

In a time-pressured world, the prospect of fruitless investments of time and attention is painful to consider. We face this problem ourselves. We are researchers working in a lab that is mandated to work with Canadian companies to enhance their use of teaching and learning technology in the workplace. A good part of our work takes the form of design experiments[1] (Brown, 1992; Collins, 1992). The method of the design experiment calls for researchers to introduce some new practice or artifact right in the target situation (i.e., a classroom, a workplace) in full knowledge that this practice or artifact probably will not work as intended. However, if properly managed, the experiment will provide valuable lessons that enable the researcher to go back to the drawing board, and incorporate these lessons into the next design iteration. Such an approach means we have a generally high tolerance for disappointing results.

... for observers steeped in the history of educational reform, it seems that there is a lot of reinventing the wheel going on in this new economy.

However, such tolerance does not mean we don't need to select our engagements carefully. We have learned to distinguish between the intelligent "failures" that teach valuable lessons, and the others that teach us little or nothing. Though we don't have to achieve success with each design experiment, we don't want to waste our time and energy in diffusion efforts that fizzle out because important pieces are missing. The same thing is true of our industry partners, only more so. Our partners are people who are in the business of diffusing teaching and learning innovations into their organizations. They have no time to waste either.

What would be helpful in this regard is something that Bereiter & Scardamalia have identified as component of expertise — the ability to select problems to work on that will yield to study, and so deepen our knowledge of some domain. Not all problems do this. Those that do are said to show promisingness (Bereiter & Scardamalia, 1993). We are developing a heuristic to help ourselves and the industry partners we collaborate with to identify innovation engagements that show signs of promisingness. The heuristic focuses attention on the presence or absence of four elements we think are critical to the success of a teaching and learning innovation. These four are Roles, Resources, Processes, and Measures. In this chapter, we present the warrants for our belief in the importance of these particular four factors, and present evidence of how the presence or absence of one or more of the elements made a difference to the outcome of some particular innovation initiatives.

■ Identifying Promising Innovation Initiatives in the Telelearning Workplace[2]

We have found it helpful to describe innovation initiatives as catching fire or fizzling out. Thus, it's not surprising that the heuristic we are developing bears a strong resemblance to the heuristic given to novice campers in the woods: "One log won't burn, two logs can't burn, three logs might burn, four logs will burn." One of the reasons four logs will burn is because each can play an important role in supporting the ignition and early combustion process. One can act as a windbreak. One can act as a reflector, and one can act as combustible material. We think the same could be said of the four elements we discuss below. Of course, once the fire is going, the distinction between these elements tends to burn away, but that's only when the fire is going. Our concern is with the start up process.

> *"One log won't burn,*
>
> *two logs can't burn,*
>
> *three logs might burn,*
>
> *four logs will burn."*

■ Roles

The importance and delineation of significant social roles in innovation efforts has been a staple of the literature on diffusion of innovation for thirty years. (Ancona & Caldwell, 1987; Hargadon & Sutton, 1997; Hargadon, 1998; Havelock, et. al., 1971; Lionberger, 1960; Rogers, 1986; Rogers, 1995; Schon, 1963). While there is wide variation as to which roles are the most important in particular contexts, there is consensus that the presence or absence of particular role-players can be decisive. For example, in describing the importance to the innovation process of having people in the situation who are in a position to lend social support to the product champion driving the innovation process, Peters and Waterman (Peters & Waterman, 1982) wrote, "This point is so important it is hard to overstress." The importance of the Roles component has to do with the importance of social networks, and of accepting that any sort of innovation initiative has to take place in a social context, in which people's behaviour is informed not just by financial and intellectual concerns, but also by social ones.

Another role component we look for is the opportunity to play the role that we ourselves are most comfortable with, that of the knowledge agent[3]. This role is akin to the role of teacher in the formulation given by Gallimore & Tharp

(Tharp & Gallimore, 1988). They offer a Vygotskian definition of teaching as providing assistance to learners at crucial moments in their zone of proximal development (Vygotskii, 1987). We find this a powerful and effective view of educational partnerships, but we believe that to label the supportive role with the word "teacher" is to burden the concept with a undesirable baggage. This is why we prefer the term knowledge agent.

Gallimore & Tharp argue that schools could and should be places where people with knowledge (e.g., teachers, principals, school supervisors) spend time with the learners (student, teacher, principal), get to know what the learners are trying to accomplish, and intervene in timely ways with information or ideas (or demonstrations of action) that enable the learners to achieve their goals. We find this view of learning fits quite well into workplace educational situations. In our view, change agents have agendas, and knowledge agents have knowledge they can and will contribute to advance those agendas. The mission of the knowledge agent is to provide this assistance to the change agent so long as it is needed. The goal is for the change agent to help the organization move toward a point where practitioners in the organization are able to continue the process on their own. At that point, new goals will emerge, which call for actions or abilities that the organization has not yet mastered. Then the cycle starts over again, with the change agent trying to achieve some goal, and the knowledge agent observing and then responding to what the change agent is trying to do.

➤ How This Idea Has Informed Practice/How Practice Has Informed This Idea

We regard as unpromising any engagement in which we are not dealing with a bonafide change agent (Rogers, 1995) who has either formal or informal institutional support for the innovation initiative. This sounds simple, but is often not easy to do. Genuine change agents are hard to identify. While it is true that many are called but few are chosen, it also seems to be true that many are assigned this responsibility but not responded to. We try to assess whether the change agent we are dealing with will be one of the genuine ones. This involves assessing whether this individual, or group of individuals, have the position and credibility within their organization needed for them to play the role of change agent successfully. It also involves in assessing whether the person we are dealing with really cares.

For example, in our involvement with a large financial services company, our initial contact with managers and officially designated "change agents" working in the division that had been set up to develop and introduce new knowledge management practices in the company. We thought we were talking to the right people, but it turned out that this was not the case. These initial discussions did not go anywhere. But then, almost by accident, we were put in touch with a manager who was working closer to the front lines, and trying to get some stuff going. He very much welcomed our involvement and support. By focusing our energies on this relationship, we able to develop a proposal that brought two graduate students into his division to do a usability study of some new com-puter-communications based tools that had been developed to support the companies sales force. This engagement turned out to be a valuable experience for all concerned.

The knowledge agent role only works, of course, if our change agent partner is prepared to acknowledge the need for some assistance. That's what we found in this case. By finding a genuine change agent who had both the authority and the passion, we were allowed to get into a situation where we could be of as-sistance to our partners. The important factor here is that we were dealing with a person who was close to the front lines of the organizations. This gave us a chance to help these people where they were hurting: not in any big, dramatic way, but in a way that provided value to all concerned, and set the stage for fur-ther engagements with this company.

■ Resources

When the goal is to start a fire that will keep burning, it is a good idea to make sure that you've got the resources at hand before plunging in. This is what the four logs heuristic is all about. It's a checklist of resources. But the checklist leaves out some important details, as most heuristics do. Four logs aren't all you need to get a fire going, but the other resources that will be needed — kin-dling, matches, a dry spot, and a supply of wood on hand to keep the fire going once it is started — are generally assumed to be present.

We consider flexibility, as defined by Bateson, to be a key resource in suc-cessful innovation engagements. Flexibility is "uncommitted capacity for change" (Bateson, 1972). We believe that this includes the resources of time and attention. By its nature, innovation implies change, and generally change of practice. Innovation requires that people stop doing one thing, and start do-ing another.

There has to be some flexibility in the system that is innovating. If there is no flexibility in the organization that is innovating, no uncommitted time or at-tention resources, the promisingness of the situation is low. This is because the new patterns of behaviour will never be able to compete[4] with old ones (Dennett, 1995). To engage in some new practice places a significant cognitive load (Sweller & Chandler, 1994) on the actor, often simultaneously with a drop off in quality and performance. If there is no slack in the system, no flexibility, the efficiency of old patterns of behaviour, patterns that are habitual and hence nearly automatic, will simply crowd out the new ones. No matter what the potential gains are of learning to touch type, or of switching to a Dvorak keyboard layout (Rogers, 1995), if there is no slack in the system to support the initial significant drop off in performance, the chances of this innovation catching on are very low. Similarly, if there is no flexibility in the system, the chances of other innovations, other changes of practice catching on, are very low.

➤ How This Idea Has Informed Practice/How Practice Has Informed This Idea

In our engagements with industry partners, we regard as promising those engagement in which we deal with someone who has either been given, or has made, time to work and consult with us. An example that shows the difference this can make is a recent engagement with the distance education unit of a large Canadian organization. The director of this unit has initiated a significant knowledge management initiative that is intended to improve the unit's ability to surface and disseminate generalizable knowledge. We were invited in early on in the initiative to observe what was going on, and to help move this process forward. This engagement turned out to be valuable for all concerned, but this value would not have emerged if the unit had been stretched so tight that no one could spend time to help us understand what we were seeing. As we developed a prime contact in that situation who had the flexibility to spend time talking to us about what was going on, this reflection time made a huge difference to the outcome for both sides. By helping us understand what they were trying to do, and where they were in the zone of proximal development, she enabled us to make a contribution that was appropriate and helpful.

In our work with partners around helping them assess the promisingness of an innovation initiative, we encourage them to assess whether there is any flexibility in the system. If there is not, if people are already up tight (Bateson, 1972) against the limits of time and attention, the large cognitive overheads of the new practice will make it uncompetitive against the automatic efficiency of the habitual. This factor seems to account for some of the early results from a knowledge management innovation one of our partners is currently pursuing. Though the idea behind this initiative seemed sound, and therefore presumably promising, the early results suggest otherwise. The innovation initiative calls for people to start investing significant amounts of time in attending meetings for the purpose of knowledge sharing. After the initial trial period of these practices, attendance at these meetings has been gradually diminishing. Our inference is that this is because the uncompetitive return on these time investments is becoming apparent to the persons involved. These project managers who work under tight deadlines, with lots of pressure from their clients. There is no slack in their system. The initiative was developed as a way of addressing these time pressures, yet the initial effect has been to increase them.

No matter how good the idea is, if there is no flexibility of time or attention that can be pried loose to attend to the new practices, workplace learning initiatives like this tend to fizzle out. This does not mean that the change agent should give up, however. It merely means that the agent should devote effort to getting the needed flexibility, the allocation of time and attention, that the initiative will need. Once the resources are in place, then the effort to light a fire can proceed with a greater likelihood of success.

■ Processes

Having the necessary resources on hand, and a clear understanding of whose job it will be to start the fire, and collect the firewood, is a good start on the road to getting a fire going. But the prospects for sustained combustion won't be good if there is no process for combining the four logs in the right place at the right time. For the combustion situation to be really promising, there must be a source of knowledge about how and when to bring the logs together. This could be a person or it could be a recipe or set of instructions in a field guide. But without such a source of procedural knowledge, chances are high that the fire will fizzle out.

Procedural knowledge enables us to know what to expect. This takes us to the crux of the issue because one of the difficulties with innovation initiatives is that people participating in them often don't know what to expect, and this makes it difficult for them to embrace the new initiative. Because such initiatives amount to a move into novel situations, there is some need to ask people to suspend judgement and to develop a new set of expectations — and yet to imagine that

No matter how good
the idea is,
if there is no flexibility
of time or attention
that can be pried loose
to attend
to the new practices,
workplace learning initiatives
like this tend
to fizzle out.

people can enter into engagement wholeheartedly without some kind of guide to what to expect is not psychologically sound. There are always some set of expectations operating (White, 1994). When expectations are unstated, or assumed not to be operative, people will form their own (Oatley, 1992; Oatley & Larocque, 1995). This makes the situation unpromising because it sets the stage for serious misunderstandings when difficulties start to arise. It is because these difficulties can have a powerful effect on the outcome of the initiative that we stress Process as one of the four factors of success for design experiments.

➤ How This Idea Has Informed Practice/How Practice Has Informed This Idea

We consider promising engagements in which both sides are willing to invest time and attention in the development of a letter of engagement for each design experiment. This is a document that spells out the goal of the engagement, and the activities that will be followed. It begins with a statement of the goals of each party, and then some brief statements about the various activities that are planned, and the contribution of each party to these activities. The document needed to be approved by both parties. This means that unworkable or unrealistic processes of engagement get flagged early on, and weeded out. What is left is a plan for a process that has been informed by the expectations and experience of both parties to the design experiment. In this way, the promisingness of the engagement is enhanced because expectations are being spelled out. If it turns out that a shared understanding of the engagement cannot be developed, we don't go forward with the engagement. We take this failure as a sign of a lack of a promising fit in the situation.

This letter not be a detailed recipe. Indeed, over-reliance on a recipe makes the situation unpromising, particularly if the recipe is being followed blindly (Wertheimer, 1959). Innovation initiatives are, by nature, novel situations, and this often means that there are no accepted procedures in place for handling this new situation. This does not mean there cannot be structure or guidance. There is a structure to the story we are in even when we don't know what the story is (Thompson, 1992). There are fairly predictable processes in play in such situations, and a knowledge and understanding of those processes will increase the likelihood of the innovation initiative being successful.

The value of this letter was shown in an engagement with one of our corporate partners. We had been invited in to witness and comment on some of the early progress of a major knowledge management initiative in this site. Because all the novelty in this situation — our presence, the new knowledge sharing practices, their culture — it was difficult to know what to expect, either of them or us. This was not problematic during the observation part of our engagement, but it became very important when it came time to communicate our perceptions, and action recommendations, to the partner.

Whenever we speak to people, they have expectations about how we will do so (White, 1994). Getting these expectations wrong can derail engagements. This is why having a process that enables people to know what to expect is so important. In this case, potential derailment, which could well have happened because of the ambiguity in the situation, was avoided because we had drawn up a letter of engagement. Thus, no expectations were disappointed. This outcome built trust between our industry partner, and us and set the stage for us to propose further engagements with them that involve much more sensitive and potentially valuable areas of their practice.

■ Measures

In building a fire, the value of procedural knowledge is highly dependent on the presence of a feedback system that informs you about where you are in the process. You have to be able to know when ignition is working, when the logs used are too wet and should be replaced, when the fire is hot enough for your purposes. If you can't tell when to take it slowly, and when to pile on the wood, the chances of success are limited. Such feedback is a product of measures of success. If you know what your goal is, and you have some form of measure that tells you how close you are getting to your goal, then you've got a feedback system.

The contribution of measures that provide feedback on progress toward clear goals is affirmed both by diffusion scholars and psychologists. Rogers wrote, "Knowledge cannot be transferred effectively unless the goals of such transfer are very clear." (Rogers, 1986). He suggests that the reason agricultural extension was such a successful method of diffusing innovations is because the measures for success were so clear: "produce more food and raise farm incomes" (Rogers, 1986). By contrast, the goals in educational situations are generally much less straightforward. Consequently, there are seldom clear measures of success because there is seldom consensus about the goals of education innovation (Rogers, 1986). By requiring clear goals and enabling feedback, the presence of

Because all the novelty in this situation — our presence, the new knowledge sharing practices, their culture — it was difficult to know what to expect, either of them or us.

Measures in the situation promotes the possibility of deep engagement in the innovation activities (Csikszentmihalyi, 1975; Csikszentmihalyi, 1993). When people can see (through the lenses of empirical measurement) that they are making progress towards a goal, they are more likely to commit energy and resources. This attracts attention and engagement, the keys to a successful diffusion initiative. This is why the presence of measures increases the promisingness of potential design experiments.

> ➤ **How This Idea Has Informed Practice/How Practice Has Informed This Idea**

We focus on identifying some clear goals in our engagements with others, and try to make them explicit in our letter of engagement. The presence of such goals focuses our attention, and that of our partners, on some fairly concrete details. This increases the promisingness of the design experiment because it means that unfocused energy will not be expended. It increases the likelihood of concentration, and as Drucker noted, concentration is crucial to business success (Drucker, 1964). Putting measures on the engagement agenda serves to put both goals and feedback on the engagement agenda. The presence of these elements significantly increases the promisingness of the engagement. It both increases the likelihood that the innovation initiative can succeed, and the chances of learning something valuable and useful from the exercise if it doesn't.

When people can see (through the lenses of empirical measurement) that they are making progress towards a goal, they are more likely to commit energy and resources.

The experiential evidence for this claim comes mainly from engagements in initiatives that fizzled out without teaching us anything particularly valuable. One of our design experiments was an attempt to create an online community of practice (Wenger, 1998) comprised of managers and consultants working in the emerging field of knowledge management. As we saw it, many of these people would be working on the leading edge, and therefore in isolation, on problems that were often peripheral to the current preoccupations of their clients and employers. We saw our role as one of creating the venue, and then sending out the invitations to attend this virtual "meeting place". Though some interesting exchanges took place at these meetings, the initiative basically fizzled out. Our post-mortem assessment of this points to the lack of any sort of metric of success around this initiative. The goal of the initiative — to build community — started off and remained vague. "Bringing people who have things in common together" was not a measurable goal. It provided none of the crispness that could focus people's attention. If we had set some more measurable goals at the beginning, our choices would have been limited, our domain of possible invitees circumscribed. But far from limiting the chances of success, we now see that the limits that such measurable goals would have placed on the effort might have increased the chances for a promising outcome. At the very least, we would have come away with more valuable lessons — possibly about the measures themselves.

■ Conclusion

In a world in which time and attention are such scarce resources, heuristics that can help us identify ahead of time the chances of our investments of time and attention yielding good results are needed. In this chapter, we have presented such a heuristic, our own "working hypothesis" for design experiments linking academic researchers to workplace communities. We realize full well that this device is in an early stage of design, and subject to revision based on experience. But whether or not it is these four factors that will ultimately guide investment of time or attention, or some others, we feel that a tool like this will prove valuable to both researchers and managers involved in the development and diffusion of innovations. This should be true whether in the field of workplace learning and teaching, or some other areas of workplace innovation. Promisingness is a generalized concern, and so any techniques that help identify it in one context should have some transferability to others.

■ Acknowledgements

Many people contributed to these thoughts and lessons reported in this chapter. Particular thanks go to Liwana Bringelson here at the University of Waterloo, and to Jim Calder, Malcolm Roberts and Janet Walker, our colleagues out in the field. Thanks also to our research-funding agency, Canada's TeleLearning Network of Centres of Excellence (TL-NCE).

Source: Thompson, J. T. & T. T. Carey. (2000). Identifying promising innovation initiatives in workplace learning and technology: Three logs might burn, four logs will burn. In Proceedings of 2000 Annual Conference of the Association of Management/International Association of Management. Project 2005: A Millennium Congress. (San Antonio, TX, August 10-12, 2000). Chesapeake, VA: Maximilian Press Publishers. Reprinted with permission from authors and Maximilian Press.

■ Endnotes

1 "Technology provides us with powerful tools to try out different designs, so that instead of theories of education, we may begin to develop a science of education. But it cannot be an analytic science like physics or psychology; rather it must be a design science more like aeronautics or artificial intelligence. For example, in aeronautics the goal is to elucidate how different designs contribute to life, drag, maneuverability, etc.. Similarly, a design science of education must determine how different designs of learning environments contribute to learning, cooperation, motivations, etc." (Collins, 1992)

2 Our focus is on the workplace, broadly construed, rather than on the organization. It is an open question as to which level of analysis is appropriate for the concerns we raise here, but certainly team and individual learning is situated in the workplace. Further, our focus is on telelearning, which we define as "connecting people and learning resources with enabling technologies".

3 The knowledge agent concept is a general one which, like that of teacher, can be broken down in numerous sub-roles: catalyst, coach, gatekeeper, broker, etc. We're working on appropriate mapping tools for these.

4 The novelist George Eliot beautifully expressed the uncompetitiveness of new practices in relation to old ones when she wrote, "Indefinite visions of ambition are weak against the ease of doing what is habitual or beguilingly agreeable, and we all know the difficulty of carrying out a resolve when we secretly long that it may be unnecessary."

■ References

Ancona, D. G., & D.F. Caldwell, "Management Issues Facing New Project Teams in High-Technology Companies." *Advances in Industrial and Labor Relations*, 4, 1987, pp. 199-221.

Bateson, G., *Ecology and Flexibility in Urban Civilization, Steps to an ecology of mind.* New York: Ballantine Books, 1972.

Bereiter, C., & M. Scardamalia, *Surpassing ourselves: An inquiry into the nature and implications of expertise.* Chicago, IL: Open Court, 1993.

Brown, A. L., "Design Experiments: Theoretical and Methodological Challenges in Creating Complex Interventions in Classroom Settings." *Journal of the Learning Sciences*, 2,(2) 1992, pp.141-178.

Collins, A., "Toward a Design Science of Education," E. Scanlon & T. O'Shea (Eds.), *New Directions in Educational Technology.* Berlin: Springer-Verlag, 1992.

Csikszentmihalyi, M., *Beyond boredom and anxiety.* New York: Harper & Row, 1975.

Csikszentmihalyi, M., *Flow: The psychology of optimal experience.* New York: Harper & Row, 1993.

Dennett, D., *Darwin's dangerous idea : Evolution and the meanings of life.* New York: Simon & Schuster, 1995.

Drucker, P., *Managing for results.* New York: Harper & Row, 1964.

Elmore, R.E., "Getting to Scale with Good Educational Practice." *Harvard Educational Review*, 66 (1),1996, pp.1-26.

Hargadon, A., & R.I. Sutton, "Technology Brokering and Innovation in a Product Development Firm. *Administrative Science Quarterly*, 42, 1997, pp. 716-749.

Hargadon, A. B., "Knowledge Brokers: A Field Study in Organizational Learning and Innovation," *Proceedings of Academy of Management*. .San Diego: Academy of Management, 1998.

Havelock, R. G., & others. (1971). *Planning for Innovation Through Dissemination and Utilization of Knowledge*. Ann Arbor, Michigan: Center for Research on Utilization of Scientific Knowledge, Institute for Social Research, University of Michigan, 1971.

Lionberger, H. F., *Adoption of new ideas and practices*. Ames: Iowa State University Press, 1960.

Oatley, K., *Best laid schemes: The psychology of emotions*. Cambridge: Cambridge University Press, 1992.

Oatley, K., & L. Larocque, "Everyday Concepts of Emotions Following Every-Other-Day Errors in Joint Plans," J. Russell & J. Fernandex-Dols (Eds.), *Everyday conceptions of emotions*. Dordrecht, The Netherlands: Kluwer Academic Publishers, 1995.

Peters, T. J., & R.S. Waterman, Jr.. *In Search of Excellence: Lessons from America's Best-Run Companies*. New York: Warner Books, 1982.

Rogers, E. M., "Models of Knowledge Transfer: Critical Perspectives. G. M. Beal, W. Dissanayake, & S. Konoshima (Eds.), *Knowledge Generation, Exchange, and Utilization*. Boulder, CO: Westview Press, 1986.

Rogers, E. M., *Diffusion of Innovations* (Fourth. ed.). New York: Free Press, 1995.

Sarason, S., *The Culture of the School and the Problem of change*. Boston: Allyn & Bacon, 1982.

Schon, D., "Champions for Radical New Inventions. *Harvard Business Review*, 41 (March-April), 1963, pp 77-86.

Sweller, J., & P. Chandler, "Why Some Material is Hard to Learn." *Cognition and Instruction*, 12 (3), 1994, pp. 185-233.

Tharp, R. G., & R. Gallimore, *Rousing Minds to Life: Teaching, Learning, and Schooling in Social Context*. Cambridge: Cambridge University Press, 1988.

Thompson, J., *What the Situation Calls For: An Essay on the Role of Stories in the Making of Meaning*. Unpublished Master's, York University, Toronto, Ontario, 1992.

Vygotskii, L. S., *The Collected Works of L. S. Vygotsky*. New York: Plenum Press, 1987.

Wenger, E., *Communities of Practice: Learning, Meaning, and Identity*. Cambridge: Cambridge University Press, 1998.

Wertheimer, M., M. Wertheimer (Ed.), *Productive thinking* (Enlarged Edition ed.). New York: Harper & Row, 1959.

White, J. B., *Acts of Hope: Creating Authority in Law, Literature, and Politics*. Chicago: University of Chicago Press, 1994.

Chapter 12

Bringing Old Ideas to New Times:
Learning Principles of Kurt Lewin Applied to Distance Education

BY STEVEN STAHL

Kurt Lewin, born in Prussia in 1890, is recognized as the founder of modern social psychology. He immigrated to the United States in 1933 and established the Research Center on Group Dynamics at the Massachusetts Institute of Technology (M.I.T.). Lewin was a pioneer of experimental social psychology and conducted numerous studies in areas including cognitive dissonance, group cooperation and competition and group dynamics. He authored over 80 articles and published eight books before he died in 1947.

Kurt Lewin articulated three essential ideas in the late 1930s and early 1940s that can be used today to improve distance education courses taught both by the Web and interactive television: (1) the significance of learners playing an active role in discovering knowledge for themselves; (2) the importance of a cohesive approach to instruction that includes cognitive, affective, and psychomotor activities to support permanent changes in attitudes, ideas, and behaviors; and (3) the powerful impact that the social environment of the learner has in supporting change.

■ *Active Learning*

Most instructors agree that learners place more belief in knowledge they have discovered on their own than in knowledge presented by others; yet all too often these same instructors fail to trust students to learn anything not explicitly stated by the instructor. This is particularly true as it is applied to two-way compressed video or one-way video interactive television systems, where instructors continue to use classroom lecture practices. All too often, instructors have no confidence that learners can discover meaning for themselves; instead, instructors perceive that lecturing is essential to ensure that students "get it." Thus, they adopt a behaviorist rather than a constructivist approach to instructional design. The instructor often becomes so focused on the desired outcome that the process by which the outcome can best be attained is forgotten or ignored. If it is true that it takes more than the mere transfer of information for attitudes, ideas, and behaviors to change, then the instructor who relies on lectures may be failing to support the very learning that leads to long-term change.

> ...*if an instructor wants students to be able to differentiate between the possible outcomes of different approaches to a situation, he/she could instruct students to examine and then modify a given scenario to improve outcomes. This would replace the kind of unilateral, non-interactive explanation that is standard in the lecture format.*

Instruction must be planned with a clear vision of what the students will do with the content presented. It is critical that students interact with the instructional content and that activities be developed to promote and support open-ended, self-directed learning. Content should never be delivered for memorization, but instead for use as a tool in planned and sequenced activities. This requires carefully planned design, respectful feedback and dialogue, and (for the instructor new to this model of instruction) a leap of faith to believe that students will come to appropriate conclusions over time. In turn, the students' learning may take the form of changed attitudes, development of new skills, and different beliefs as to the likely consequences of a given action; all of these influence the learners' daily decision-making in future endeavors.

For example, if an instructor wants students to be able to differentiate between the possible outcomes of different approaches to a situation, he/she could instruct students to examine and then modify a given scenario to improve outcomes. This would replace the kind of unilateral, non-interactive explanation that is standard in the lecture format. The scenario could be illustrated through a role-playing exercise, a story, or an illustration of a true historical event.

Throughout the process, students would discuss their perceptions of antici-pated changes and reflect on why such changes might occur. Learners would en-gage in a wide-ranging exploration rather than a search for "the right answer." The instructor's role would thus become one of questioner, promoting deeper student examination than would be likely without facilitation.

An instructor in a Web-based environment might facilitate such a dialogue over a two-week period and require students to make references to outside re-sources. In a synchronous environment such as interactive television, the process might occur over a 30-minute period and be based, in part, on previ-ously assigned readings. This process is in sharp contrast to a behaviorist model that assumes that the goal of instruction is to transfer knowledge from expert to learner (Leidner & Jarvenpaa, 1995). A constructivist model respects learners as decision-makers in their own learning, and it supports the confi-dence of the participants, since their personal concerns are validated and ex-plored with peers and the instructor.

■ A Cohesive Approach

Lewin wrote that a piecemeal approach to guiding learners to accept new ideas, attitudes, and behaviors is ineffective. Instead, a cohesive approach must be utilized to support changes in cognition, affect, and behavior. From an instructional perspective, the implementation of this principle seems difficult in a distance environment; it requires instructional designers to plan cogni-tively challenging tasks, address the affective issues that stimulate learner recognition of the need for change, and provide opportunities for action. More-over, motivational aspects must be included in instruction. This writer takes ex-ception with authors who place emphasis on the importance of keeping activi-ties enjoyable, exciting, and agreeable (Moore & Kearsley, 1996). Engagement need not necessarily be fun or agreeable for learning to occur. For example, if instruction is aimed at encouraging firefighters to take steps to improve safety in their work environment, then the instruction must stress that the failure to act responsibly may result in tragedy. In order to obtain the desired impact, co-hesive learning strategies — even if they are not particularly enjoyable — must be employed. For example, an instructor might initiate dialogue among learn-ers about actual serious accidents and their causes or show videos of tragic events, followed by other reflective assignments.

To promote active learning, the instructional designer must identify how learners will use their bodies to solidify the learning. In the example above, learners could be asked to physically examine a potential work site and identify potential hazards. Even simple tasks that require students to move around the room-to join different groupings, to post or manipulate information or materials — can have a significant impact upon learning. Failure to address all three of these areas (cognitive, affective, and physical) in every lesson plan results in less than maximal learning outcomes.

■ The Impact of the Social Environment

Lewin theorized that before changes in ideas, attitudes, and behavior will occur, modifications in a learner's perception of self and his/her social environment are essential. He also argued that it is easier to create change in a social context than individually. These principles are supported by others, including Fischer (1997), Brown (1993), Bruffee (1993), Slavin (1990) and Newcomb (1962); they challenge the instructor to create among learners a social environment that supports self-confidence and the perception that change is occurring and accepted within the learning environment. This requires both time and planned interaction among participants.

As more dependable, high-quality desktop video conferencing equipment becomes available, additional options will develop. Through dialogue, students can negotiate and renegotiate meaning as a community of learners attempting to reconcile conflicting perceptions and assumptions.

A preliminary step to creating a community of learners is establishing the foundation for a respectful, accepting, and caring environment (Vella, 1995). With preparation, instructors can create conditions that give students the freedom to experiment with new behaviors, ideas, and attitudes in a social environment. This social environment can be face-to-face as in video conferencing, voice-to-voice as in an audio bridge, or through synchronous and/or asynchronous chat such as an Internet mailing lists, discussion boards, or Internet Relay Chat (IRC).

As more dependable, high-quality desktop video conferencing equipment becomes available, additional options will develop. Through dialogue, students can negotiate and renegotiate meaning as a community of learners attempting to reconcile conflicting perceptions and assumptions (Brown, 1993). Students' questioning of viewpoints and theories and the critical analysis of cause and effect can support rich learning experiences and should be encouraged. Though it can be challenging to accomplish in distance environments, the opportunity exists to encourage group sharing that supports individual responsibility and distributed learning.

Key to such an environment is respect (Vella, 1995): respect among learners, between learners and instructor(s), and for the community in which the learners are embedded. This means conveying the attitude that everyone present is there to learn, to practice, and to make mistakes. Respect can be achieved in any form of distance learning that permits collaboration among participants.

The education community continues to experience an increasing shift from face-to-face to distance learning environments. This qualitative change will be facilitated if we incorporate the teachings of earlier thinkers in adult learning theory. Lewin stressed the importance of active learning, cohesive instruction, and social environment to support learning that leads to permanent change. If these ideas are adhered to, we will come to see active learning not as a supplement to lecture, but as the primary mode of instruction. Cohesive instruction can be viewed as systems theory applied to the micro-world of instructional design and teaching. The effective use of social connectivity in distance instruction will keep distance education a viable learning environment.

Source: Steven Stahl, "Bringing Old Ideas to New Times: Learning Principles of Kurt Lewin Applied to Distance Education," Technology Source, *March 1999. Reprinted with permission of the author.*

■ References

Brown, A., D. Ash, M. Rutherford, K. Naka-gawa, A. Gordon, and J. Campione. "Distributed Expertise in the Classroom," Salomon, G. (Ed.), Distributed Cognitions: *Psychological and Educational Considerations*, Cambridge, UK: Cambridge University Press, 1993.

Bruffee, K. (Ed.) *Collaborative Learning: Higher Education, Interdependence, and the Authority of Knowledge*. Baltimore: Johns Hopkins University Press, 1993.

Fischer, G., "Distributed Cognition, Learning Webs, and Domain-Oriented Design Environments., 1997. Retrieved February 10, 1999 from the World Wide Web: http://www-cscl95.indiana.edu/cscl95/fischer.html.

Leidner, D., & S. Jarvenpaa, "The use of Information Technology to Enhance Management School Education: A Theoretical View." *MIS Quarterly*, 19 (3), 1995, pp. 265-286.

Moore, M., & G. Kearsley, *Distance Education: A Systems View*. Belmont, CA: Wadsworth Publishing Company, 1996.

Newcomb, T., "Student Peer-Group Influence," T. Newcomb & E. Wilson (Eds.), *The American College: A Psychological and Social Interpretation of the Higher Learning*. New York: Wiley Press, 1962.

Slavin, R., *Cooperative Learning: Theory, Research, and Practice*. Englewood Cliffs, NJ: Prentice Hall, 1990.

Vella, J., *Training Through Dialogue: Promoting Effective Learning and Change with Adults*. San Francisco, CA: Jossey Bass, 1995.

Chapter 13

If You Got IT
Flaunt IT:
Construction
of a Paperless Classroom

By Joseph Slowinski

I'm always amazed at the reactions I receive from colleagues when I announce that I teach a course that uses no paper. Upon hearing of an actual implementation of a paperless classroom, many practicing educators tend to "freeze up," replete with dumbfounded expressions and interesting facial contortions that finally lead to a reflective response of "huh?" At this point, after several such encounters, I realize that a material-free classroom sounds alien to most[1]. Yet the reality of a paperless classroom is not so far-fetched. Many educators have access to technologies that could make it a reality. For example, a paperless learning environment can be accomplished with no more than an Internet connection and either Netscape Communicator or Microsoft Internet Explorer, both available for free on the World Wide Web (WWW). I truly believe that most educators see the potential value in information technology as a learning tool but they just don't believe it is possible to realize a paperless classroom. A paperless classroom not only is feasible for educators but more importantly; it can be a catalyst for educational reform. In addition, as we approach an Information Age, technologically competent teachers are needed to prepare children for the future.

As we enter the new millennium, educators are vested with the task of preparing students for the emergence of an information society. For example, as information technology (IT) becomes further embedded in society, students will need computer skills in their jobs. Approximately 60% of all future jobs will require knowledge of computers (Slowinski, 1999). Yet, many jobs remain unfilled due to a lack of unqualified applicants. For example, a recent report, released by the Information Technology Association of America in April of this year, "Bridging the Gap: Information Technology Skills for a New Millennium," revealed that an estimated 850,000 IT jobs will remain unfilled this year revealing a disturbing trend. IT-related positions in 2000 are more than double the number of 1998 openings (346,000) and quadruple the value of 1997 (190,000).

... a lack of experience and use of computer technology are the most distinct predictors of technophobia — the fear of computer use.

Although most educators won't directly teach students how to write computer programming languages or how to use software applications, they can begin to play an important role in preparing students with technology skills through providing the opportunity to use and practice skills in their classrooms. This process is critical. For instance, a lack of experience and use of computer technology are the most distinct predictors of technophobia — the fear of computer use (Rosen & Weil, 1995). Students need exposure and the opportunity to engage in productive activities using computer technology. One such method is the development of a paperless classroom.

Consequently, in this chapter, in an effort to facilitate a dialog on the future of education, I explore this new classroom: the paperless classroom.

■ What is a Paperless Classroom?

A paperless class is a course that operates by reducing the amount of physical material exchanges between teacher and student. For example, through the utilization of information technology, students submit assignments virtually with the aid of the Internet and other software. But, what is needed for a paperless classroom? A paperless learning environment involves a fundamental shift from the traditional physical exchange of materials between teacher and student to a symbolic or virtual exchange[2]. Through the utilization of information technology, students locate resources, communicate through e-mail, conduct research through the WWW and submit assignments electronically to the teacher. Since a paperless classroom is dependent upon the amount of technology available in the school and community, teachers can discuss the use of technology with students and parents to determine the appropriate level of a paperless environment for their class.

■ Construction of a Paperless Learning Environment

The paperless classroom serves as a metaphor for a technology-rich and knowledge-laden learning environment. Since the inception of the WWW in 1989, the information super highway has been actively engaged in paving the road to an information age. Through the increased use of the Internet in American classrooms, students have the opportunity to gain access to an unprecedented amount of knowledge: a virtual library open 24 hours a day, 365 days a year. I contend that this information access can lead to a fundamental shift in the role of teacher and student in the learning process. Due to the expansive knowledge base available online, teachers can become facilitators of learning rather than the sole disseminators of information in the classroom. Yet this requires a radical paradigm shift in daily classroom practice. The following describes the fundamental elements of a paperless classroom.

➤ E-mail Rapport

As a fundamental part of the process, a paperless classroom must begin before students arrive physically in the classroom. In an effort to counter some of the initial expected resistance (of which I discuss in a later cautionary note), I send e-mail to students prior to their arrival in the class. Through this approach, students and parents who are likely to resist are provided with some initial time to complain and ponder before entering the classroom. Expectations for a technology-rich learning environment must establish computer-oriented expectations. By obtaining student e-mail addresses, a distribution list can be constructed that serves to set the tone for classroom communications. By contacting students prior to arriving in the physical space, a teacher communicates expectations for computer use in the class.

As a fundamental part of the process, a paperless classroom must begin before students arrive physically in the classroom.

E-mail offers communication that takes place between each student and teacher outside of the physical territory of the classroom. This allows students to ponder and ask questions whenever they are learning outside of the school. There is a cognitive benefit to the learner when they ponder the issue and construct the question. In a traditional learning environment, a student would realize they have a question and then move on planning to ask the question the following day. Yet, there is a chance they will forget the issue. E-mail offers learning as well as communication. In my course, I respond to e-mail messages as soon as I receive them. These student messages are my priority when I login to my account. I know that students desire to resolve their problems through the aid of my advice and suggestions, and I am sensitive to their needs. Furthermore, through a speedy e-mail reply, students begin to realize that they are valued and respected. This in turn promotes the use of e-mail as a communication device. If teachers do not respond regularly, students are far less likely to communicate and thus not use e-mail.

➤ Online Syllabus

In traditional classrooms, contact and knowledge acquisition is often restricted to the physical classroom space. In the paperless classroom, an online syllabus ensures potential access to information and communication 24 hours a day by students or parents. This is especially valuable for students who are ill. An online syllabus should include a number of items: teacher contact information, class expectations, class requirements, assignments, a help page, and an updated links page. Yet, resources are limited without a strategy. An effective use of an online syllabus is to align course/class content with online resources. This alignment can facilitate self-efficacy in learners by providing electronic resources that foster their learning.

In the paperless classroom, an online syllabus ensures potential access to information and communication 24 hours a day by students or parents.

In addition, an online syllabus can promote multiculturalism as well as access for minority language parents. On my class syllabus, I have integrated a link to the Alta Vista Babelfish Web-based translator to provide class information in five different languages (e.g., Spanish, Italian, German, Portuguese, French). Through the inclusion of this translator, a teacher offers access to the syllabus to minority language students or parents. In addition, the teacher communicates to minority language parents that she or he is interested in learning for all students regardless of their family background.

■ Asynchronous Discussion Software

In addition to e-mail, the use of an asynchronous discussion software package promotes paperless interchange. Alta Vista Forum is a Web-based discussion software package that allows students to post messages 24 hours a day.

Asynchronous communication offers the benefit of allowing the student to re-spond when it is convenient for him or her to do so. In my class, I utilize Alta Vista Forum to facilitate group discus-sions and reflections. Normally, students read an essay and compose a reflection essay to the forum. Since the forum is Web-based, students can access the page through the WWW. In addition, students can read peer reflections on issues. Through this process, the illusionary and hidden notions of peer work are offered to the class community. Through reading, reflecting and critiquing peer work, stu-dents learn how to improve their own writing while learning how to offer constructive criticism.

> *Traditionally, teachers have held power and authority over students resulting in an inherently unfair and undemocratic system of education.*

■ Why a Paperless Classroom?

One potential argument for a shift to a paperless classroom is the reduction of paper use. Yet, I won't posit an environmental argument here. Although tempting and perhaps politically correct to do so, I must resist. Since I print out materials from web sites in my own research, I would be a hypocrite to hide be-hind such a green facade. Rather, I will put forth the notion that a paperless classroom can lead to educational reform through altering the power structure in the classroom.

Traditionally, teachers have held power and authority over students result-ing in an inherently unfair and undemocratic system of education. Since teachers were the holders of an established body of knowledge that needed to be transmitted to the student, knowledge was synonymous with control and power. Teachers dictated what was learned, from where it was learned, how it was learned and how quickly it was learned. Yet, due to a global infor-mation flow available in cyberspace, these traditional roles should not be maintained today.

For example, as we enter the new millennium, it is impossible for a teacher or textbooks to possess all available knowledge; no longer should we view edu-cators as the only repository of information. Through the WWW, students can seek out information on various curriculum areas without relying completely on the educator for this knowledge. This can empower both teachers and students by freeing them from the traditional roles of teacher as disseminator and student as recipient.

■ *Learning in this Paperless Environment*

As a teacher shifts to a paperless learning environment, the fundamental roles of teacher and student blur. In an effort to offer a method of operating a paperless classroom, I suggest a series of ideas and procedures that can be used to develop a learning environment. In many ways, these suggestions are modeled after the scientific method but are directly adopted from Black and McClintock's (1995) Interpretation Construction model.

1. *Students begin the learning process by thinking about topics from their own experiences.* From their experiences, students develop hypotheses about the topic area. What do they think is true? Why did or does this occur? If the student has no knowledge, then they jump immediately to step two.

2. *Students use the* WWW *to search for information about the topic area.* First, students need to think about where they would find such information. In addition to helping students learn how to use a search engine, the teacher aids in developing logical thinking skills. In regard to initial assertions, this research information is used to develop or refine their initial hypotheses that have been generated related to the topic area. In the paperless classroom, students can e-mail questions to scholars or other experts on the topic areas. Surprisingly, most people feel more comfortable responding to e-mail questions.

3. *During the research phase, the classroom teacher should work with students on developing research and evaluation skills.* Black and McClintock refer to this as the cognitive apprenticeship phase. Through working with an expert researcher, the classroom teacher and students gain a better comprehension about how to search for information. In addition, the teacher can aid the student in evaluating web sites for content. Through the aid of the classroom teacher, students can develop a keen sense of the value of Web information. Students can learn to ask critical questions about Web information. Who is the author? Who supports this web site? Is the information valid? Can it be validated from other information?

4. *After completing research and refining their assumptions, students come together in small groups to discuss their hypotheses and research that supports these assertions.* Through com-

munication and discussion, students are exposed to a variety of ideas and perspectives. These various perspectives help the student view diversity of opinion. Through this social discourse, students can attempt to arrive at a consensus. More importantly, the teacher can assist the student in the importance of tolerating different ideas and debating in humane ways.

5. *This process is completed and can be facilitated for the next topic area that is dictated through the curriculum.* At this stage, a teacher can choose to have a summative evaluation. Yet, a cautionary note should be considered. Since students have developed their own hypotheses and conducted their own research, assessment can be gauged from an objective body of facts in addition to their own perspective of debatable truths. Formative assessment and feedback are offered to students as they proceed with learning.

> ... *students are empowered to seek out information while the teacher is a mentor in developing the student's ability to learn and acquire information and knowledge.*

Through the utilization of this method, students are empowered to seek out information while the teacher is a mentor in developing the student's ability to learn and acquire information and knowledge. The classroom teacher's role has changed yet the importance of the teacher has increased. Rather than disseminating content area knowledge, the teacher works to help students develop metacognitive skill; skills that will be needed as we progress further in an information society, a society where students possess the ability to independently learn new information. A paperless classroom environment provides such training.

■ *Cautionary Note 1: Initial Student Resistance to the Paperless Environment*

In the process of developing a paperless learning environment, several realizations will aid the innovative teacher in moving from a more traditional approach to the virtual paperless classroom. To put it bluntly, innovation often evokes resistance. For example, perceptions of what good teaching is and what appropriate practices are will initially lead to potential resistance from administrators, colleagues, and parents. Initially, colleagues and parents will be skeptical of the possibility of a paperless classroom. Since most teachers' and parents' experiences remain embedded in the use of physical materials in the classroom, there will be resistance to the shift toward a paperless-driven teacher.

In addition, when students arrive in any classroom they will also carry with them a set of socially constructed assumptions of how the class and teacher should operate. Traditionally, this has entailed the assumption that the teacher is the disseminator of knowledge and the student is the recipient of this knowledge. Consequently, if a teacher attempts to break from this model of teaching then a lack of congruency between what is expected and what is reality occurs. Often this provokes resistance on behalf of the student. Students may also perceive the paperless practitioner as inferior to the traditional model. A paperless classroom can be empowering to the student and requires an investment on behalf of the student in his/her own learning. Resistance and individual perceptions are issues that will initially undermine your efforts, especially in schools where other teachers are not striving for the integration of technology in the learning process. As you proceed in your quest to the paperless classroom be aware that ideological perceptions will operate as a barrier.

After resistance, teachers should be actively involved in modeling the paperless classroom process with students. Initially, teachers and students can participate in a large group and proceed through the process together. As the initial cycle is completed, teachers can slowly wean the students off of traditional schooling to the more empowering paperless classroom. Teachers can fulfill curriculum requirements by providing the topic areas and content students need to explore. Yet, students will be actively engaged in uncovering the information rather than being feed the material by the teacher. More importantly, students will be exposed to periphery material and a diversity of perspectives that one teacher cannot provide.

■ *Cautionary Note 2: Issues of Health*

Throughout the chapter I have praised information technology and the potential for developing a paperless classroom. In conclusion, I want to offer a cautionary note to readers. Teachers who use information technology in a classroom should be aware of the potential health hazards that could result from adopting technology in day-to-day operations. For example, an educator who opts for a paperless classroom will surely promote the use of technology for students in the classroom, as well as in the home. These educators must be aware that repetitive use of a keyboard is a potential threat for Carpal Tunnel Syndrome. In addition, eye, back, and neck strain can result from repetitive use of a computer. But, with the knowledge of ergonomics, a teacher can design a classroom setting in a manner that promotes safe computer use. If you choose to implement a paperless classroom, then acquire a working knowledge of ergonomics and set-up your classroom in a healthy manner that minimizes these potential health threats. Knowledge of ergonomic principles can greatly reduce the risks of discomfort or injury.

■ Conclusion

The adaptation of the paperless classroom is not an educational panacea but, more importantly, a potential catalyst for improved learning conditions in schools. Through electronic sources, the learning process is removed from the rigidity of the physical classroom space and placed into the world's knowledge base. Consequently, students learn, communicate, and submit their assignments anywhere and at anytime rather than being constrained by physical materials and the classroom itself. More importantly, teachers and students become freed from the restrictions of the traditional roles of teacher as disseminator and student as recipient.

Free Tools to Support a Paperless Classrooom	
WebEx	http://www.webex.com
Zkey	http://zkey.com
HearMe	http://www.hearme.com
TalkMe	http://www.talkme.com
Evoke	http://www.evoke.com
Free Disk Space	http://www.freediskspace.com
Third Voice	http://www.thirdvoice.com
Babylon	http://www.babylon.com
FreeTranslation	http://www.freetranslation.com
Alta Vista Babelfish	http://babelfish.altavista.com

Source: Joe Slowinski, "If You Got IT Flaunt IT: Construction of a Paperless Classroom," WebNet Journal April-June 2000 (www.aace.org/pubs/webnet). Reprinted with permission from the author.

■ References

Black, J.B., & R.O. McClintock, "An Interpretation Construction Approach to Constructivist Design." B. Wilson (Ed.). *Constructivist Learning Environment.* Englewood Cliffs, NJ: Educational Technology Publications, 1995. Available online at: http://www.it.columbia.edu

Blumenstyk, G., Study warns of a shortage of peopie trained for jobs in technology. *The Chronicle of HVW Education,* 1997.

Information Technology Association of America, *Bridging the Gap: Information Technology Skills for a New Millennium.* Arlington, VA: Author, 2000.

Information Technology of America, "Help Wanted 2: A Call for Collaborative Action for the New Millennium, 1998, [Online]. Available at: http://www.itaa.org.

Information Technology of America, "Help Wanted: The IT Workforce Gap at the Dawn of a New Century, 1997, [Online]. Available at: http://www.kaa.org.

Rosen, L.D., & M.M. Weil, "Computer Availability, Computer Experience and Technophobia Among Public School Teachers. *Computers in Human Behavior* 17 (l) 1995, pp. 9 -31.

Slowinski, J., "Internet in America's Schools: Potential Catalysts for Policy Makers. First Monday, 4 (1) 1999, [Online]. Available at: http://www.firstmonday.dk.

■ Endnotes

1 In my class, I utilize technology that aims all assignments and communication to occur through virtual symbolic exchange. No physical exchange (e.g.. submitting a disk) is necessary. In some classrooms, students could submit assignments through computer disks. This would not be a virtual exchange but a material exchange.

2 Virtual exchange involves the exchange of information without physical materials. For example, the use of asynchronous communication tools to submit essay reflections.

Chapter 14

Enhancing Professional Education through Virtual Knowledge Networks

By Charles Morrissey

"There is no point in asking which came first, the educational explosion of the last 100 years or the management that put this knowledge to productive use. Modern management and modern enterprise could not exist without the knowledge base that developed societies have built. But equally, it is management, and management alone, that makes effective all this knowledge and these knowledgeable people. The emergence of management has converted knowledge from social ornament and luxury into the true capital of any economy."

— Peter Drucker (1989)

Organizations are in the midst of adapting to enormous changes brought about by technological breakthroughs in computers and communication. Accelerated particularly by continuing developments in collaborative technologies known as "groupware," these breakthroughs are having a profound impact on the management process. They are also stimulating — in this, the "Network Era," as it has been dubbed by leading scholars (Nolan & Croson, 1995) — a transition from a hierarchical to a virtual workplace. In the latter, dispersed team members from multiple disciplines work cooperatively to adapt to competitive situations (Townsend, DeMarie, & Hendrickson, 1998). They communicate via electronic meetings, which have become commonplace in our intensely competitive and global marketplace. At the heart of these new, team-based information systems is the objective of capturing, organizing, and distributing the intellectual capital of the firm for which the team members work. Academicians describe this process as "knowledge management" (Cole, 1998).

The knowledge management movement creates new challenges and opportunities for the field of professional education, which would do well to develop an educational equivalent to the virtual workplace. The rapid expansion of the Internet as a potential course delivery platform, combined with the increasing interest in life-long learning, has created a significant opportunity for graduate programs to adapt to technological advances. Responding to these advances, however, will require a rigorous reexamination of the traditional university's bricks-and-mortar delivery system. This chapter examines how traditional universities can enrich the student learning experience — and become more responsive to stakeholders — by developing what I call a Virtual Knowledge Network.

Corporations, government and non-profit agencies spend hundreds of millions of dollars each year on formal education programs for management personnel.

■ Professional Education Programs

Corporations, government and non-profit agencies spend hundreds of millions of dollars each year on formal education programs for management personnel. These programs range from short, single-subject seminars to complete management degree programs. Agency employees take almost all of these courses in some form of "limited residency" so that they still may fulfill their responsibilities in their respective organizations. As part-time students, the managers-in-training move back and forth between the culture of industry and that of the classroom, where they develop new relationships with people from other disciplines and firms. Graduates of these programs often attribute much of their learning to their interactions with classroom peers, and they often attempt to maintain peer relationships throughout their careers.

In many ways, the environment of these management training programs is analogous to that of the virtual workplace. Consider, for example, the fact that many agency-sponsored education programs rely heavily on case method teaching, a form of instruction that requires students to prepare for class in study group meetings. Often the topic at these meetings is a case analysis task, an assignment in which students must examine a given problem and recommend a course of corrective action within a limited time frame. Each student brings his/her own unique expertise to the analysis, which is then critiqued in class by the instructor and often by professional guest speakers. Thus, like the multi-discipline, virtual teams operating in today's professional organizations, these student groups are shaped by the individual members' skills and by input from knowledgeable sources.

■ *The Role of Information Technology*

It is important to recognize, however, that professional education classrooms also differ significantly from the virtual workplace. Electronic meetings, for example, are rare; communication between instructors and students remains largely face-to-face in scheduled locations at scheduled times. Moreover, instructors employ technology tools much less frequently than do members of virtual workteams. Despite a rapidly growing investment in information technology infrastructure in most management schools (Green, 1998), IT is not being aligned with the learning process.

This is a foolish omission, for research shows that collaborative technologies can improve the quality of learning (Morrissey, 1997). In accordance with that fact, higher education libraries are rapidly expanding the availability of online, digital document databases that support student and faculty research and that enhance professional curriculum development. With ProQuest Direct, for example,

... higher education libraries are rapidly expanding the availability of online, digital document databases that support student and faculty research and that enhance professional curriculum development.

instructors can execute a periodical search (by subject, journal or specific article title), use the search results to augment course content materials, then electronically distribute these materials any time, anywhere. Traditional text publishers, such as Harvard Business School Publishing, now provide similar Internet-based delivery systems of their content. Moreover, Internet software developers are introducing inexpensive video and audio transmission tools that enable access to "same time, different place" meetings such as lectures at distant universities and online conferences. When professional programs integrate these tools, they not only provide a richer curriculum, but also create the opportunity to implement a Virtual Knowledge Network.

■ The Virtual Knowledge Network

In a Virtual Knowledge Network, students and faculty are part of a continuous, online learning spectrum that is marked by unlimited interaction; contact with a vast array of knowledge resources is no longer restricted by place, distance, or format. These knowledge resources include faculty, students, alumni, and community members. Through collaborative technologies like those described above, the Network enables the seamless flow of discussion and documents, enriches the delivery of core curriculum concepts, and most importantly, meets the specific educational interests of individual students.

Faculty members assume the role of true knowledge managers by facilitating "knowledge groups," a new form of the traditional study group (Brufee, 1993). Knowledge group membership can be extended to students in other classes, alumni, faculty, and university partners. Participants in this new learning environment purchase course materials through electronic commerce. Alumni and community partners provide financial support through annual subscriptions (Head, 1999).

■ The Virtual Knowledge Network in Practice: A Scenario

Imagine that Cathy, a 35 year-old marketing manager from an early-stage pharmaceutical firm, is a student in Professor M's class. Cathy has worked in marketing for 12 years; she started as a sales representative in a major medical firm after earning a bachelor's degree in economics. She has been with her current firm for the past eight years and has been given increasingly complex responsibilities in product management. Cathy's current job assignment is to coordinate a team that will launch a new product about to be approved by the U.S. Food and Drug Administration (FDA).

Professor M's 15-week course includes 10 traditional, face-to-face sessions; the other five sessions are conducted online. Cathy's study group for this course includes three other students, an alumnus of her program, and an associate from her firm. She also is a member of a five-person group working on a collaborative thesis project. Professor M mentions that the university's executive program has had a number of pharmaceutical industry students. Through a search of the alumni database, Cathy finds an alumnus who recently was named CEO of a new venture in the industry. Through a search of the current student database, she identifies a student in another class who is part of a group studying post-FDA approval litigation. Cathy invites both of these individuals to participate in the thesis group's electronic meetings. The alumnus, in turn, provides Cathy's group with access to his firm's monthly "open forum" Web conference, which is designed to keep clients informed about product developments. Finally, Cathy searches the faculty database and finds a faculty member who is a consultant on FDA regulations.

The university is the heart of rich content, expertise and knowledge exchanges. It now has the opportunity to enhance this role by employing knowledge management concepts as the basis for its IT investment

Later, Cathy accesses the University Web site, which is hosting a joint law/medical school conference on new pharmaceutical advertising regulations. She electronically "attends" the conference, then archives it for later viewing with her study group and colleagues.

■ Conclusion

This brief scenario highlights the way in which a university must leverage its increasing investment in IT if it truly is to serve its stakeholders. The university is the heart of rich content, expertise and knowledge exchanges. It now has the opportunity to enhance this role by employing knowledge management concepts as the basis for its IT investment (Privateer, 1999).

However, this new focus will require changes in organizational structure and processes (Miles, et al, 1997). University executives would do well to follow the example of selected industries that have been through the same transformative process and successfully developed virtual workteams (Weill, 1998). Administrators must be receptive to change and approach curriculum structure and delivery systems with a "clean slate" mentality. They must encourage alumni to remain part of the university "community" long after they have graduated. And they must allow faculty to be at the heart of this transformation, acting as "knowledge managers" in a new structure that transcends time and space in order to serve a broader and more technologically-savvy constituency. Universities that recognize the strategic opportunity to implement Virtual Knowledge Networks will enjoy a significant competitive advantage in the next century.

Source: Charles Morrissey, "Enhancing Professional Education through Virtual Knowledge Networks," Technology Source, July/August 1999. Reprinted with permission of the author.

■ References

Brufee, K. P., *Collaborative Learning*. Baltimore: John Hopkins Press, 1993.

Cole, R. E., Ed., "Knowledge and the Firm: Special issue." *California Management Review* 40(3) 1998.

Drucker, P., *The New Realities*. New York: Harper and Row, 1989.

Green, K. C., "Colleges Struggle with IT Planning." *The Campus Computing Project Newsletter*. Claremont, CA: Center for Educational Studies, Claremont Graduate University, 1998.

Head, N. W., "Higher Education: A Key Partner in the Information System Knowledge Supply Chain," Jayesh Prasad (Ed.), *Proceedings of the Association of Computing Machinery: Special Interest Group Computer Personnel Research (SIGCPR)*, New York: Association of Computing Machinery, 1999, April, pp. 279-282.

Miles, R. E., C.C. Snow, J.A. Mathews & H.J. Coleman, "Organizing in the Knowledge Age: Anticipating the Cellular Form." *Academy of Management Executive* 11(4), 7-19.

Morrissey, C. A., "The Impact of Groupware on the Case Method in Management Education." Unpublished Ph.D. dissertation, Claremont Graduate University, 1997.

Nolan, R. & D.C. Croson, *Creative Destruction*. Boston: HBS Press, 1995.

Privateer, P. M., "Academic Technology and the Future of Higher Education: Strategic Paths Taken and Not Taken." *The Journal of Higher Education* 70(1) 1999, January , pp. 60-79.

Townsend, A., S.M. DeMarie & A.R. Hendrickson, "Virtual Teams: Technology and the Workplace of the Future." *Academy of Management Executive* 12(3) 1998, pp. 17-29.

Weill, P. & M. Broadbent, *Leveraging the New Infrastructure: How Market Leaders Capitalize on Information Technology*. Boston: HBS Press, 1998.

Chapter 15

Building a Foundation for Connected Learning

By Peggi Munkittrick

Out of necessity, most institutions offering connected learning programs have focused on the creation and delivery of course content. Now that institutions and vendors are gaining more experience in this growing field, it is evident that the programs need to be far more encompassing. Following are six elements that are necessary to build a truly effective and collaborative-connected learning environment. (Note:, SCT uses the term "connected learning" to refer to the delivery mechanism and/or the relationship of connecting populations regardless of their location.)

■ One: infrastructure and support

The first, and perhaps most obvious, element is the foundation — the infrastructure. The network infrastructure must ensure worldwide, high-bandwidth access to course resources for an institution's students and its instructors. Adequate hardware and software servers must be available to "host" online courses and course components. In addition, hosting support services must be available. These should include a student and faculty help desk service, online help assistance and training. Both the servers and the network require experienced management to ensure a high degree of reliability and quality, 24x7.

Institutions must also consider that some students will not have access to state-of-the-art technology. Thus, they should consider taking advantage of off-line software applications that help free up network bandwidth and phone lines. Remote replication applications synchronize updates made offline with content already on the server. Also, high-bandwidth media such as CD-ROM work in tandem with the Internet for increased speed and seamless course navigation.

■ Two: an administrative system and the ability to do data sharing

Vital to student services, the data currently housed within an institution's administrative system is vital to quality student services. Thus, it is important that data flow seamlessly and in real time between connected learning applications and an institution's central administrative database. This requires a standard interface (API) to leverage access to the administrative system from other course delivery technologies. This makes the administration of connected learning courses simple, straightforward, and without redundant data entry. From single sign-on of registration to grades, data is entered only once. Without this integration, faculty or their staff will be required to perform redundant administrative tasks.

An integrated system also enables an institution to provide connected learning students with the same level of customer service as on-campus students.

Real time data sharing also improves service to connected-learning students. For example, students can begin reviewing course materials as soon as they initiate the sign-up process rather than wait 24 hours or longer while their registration information is entered and they are cleared for access.

An integrated system also enables an institution to provide connected learning students with the same level of customer service as on-campus students. For example, most learners today do not have remote access to libraries, bookstores, personal and career counseling or technical support. These services are so lacking to remote learners that the U.S. Department of Education has labeled them "orphan services." Research and product development is under way in this area by the Western Cooperative for Educational Telecommunications and SCT. The Cooperative and SCT recently received a Learning Anytime Anyplace Partnership (LAAP) grant for US$700,000 to create a host of new Web-based student services. This is the first national effort to define and provide tools for addressing the full range of services that must be provided in a learning anytime, any place format for connected learners.

■ Three: a customized portal

The third critical element is a portal for access to, and delivery of, course content and associated resources. Through a single Web logon through any browser, faculty and students can access the resources and data they need. For students, this could be the library and bookstore. For faculty, the resources would include advanced reporting and grading tools. Of course, all the necessary collaborative and instructional tools must also be accessible.

This single logon, coupled with the integration to the administrative database, ensures the security of critical features such as accessing courses, passing of student registration information, posting of grades, and accuracy of tracking progress.

■ Four: tools for content development, and content course management and course taking

These tools are the most widely used and available today. Faculty are demanding content development tools that are powerful, yet easy-to-use with features like WYSIWYG editing, drag-and-drop reorganization and customizable learning environments. To help faculty new to connected instruction, some software solutions offer outline paradigms that give instructors one place to outline their courses, specify objectives, add tests and question banks, define glossary terms, write course content and add rich media.

Additional faculty resources available today include course management tools such as easy-to-use testing and certification features, progress updates, and easy access for help and questions.

Required content management tools include statistical reports, templates, style sheets and dynamic assessment engines. The latter are becoming increasingly important as people inside and outside of higher education attempt to gauge the effectiveness of connected learning. With a built-in assessment engine, faculty can write tests that direct learners to appropriate course material highlighting relevant information. When learners offer incorrect responses, the application can respond with instructor feedback, and provide appropriate materials for remediation.

Standard course-taking tools include a user interface, bookmarks, search and automatic résumé. Collaboration tools should include chat rooms, e-mail and discussion groups.

■ Five: learning object repositories

This is another under-developed area of connected learning. Yet, its importance is critical in order to make quality content widely accessible and allow institutions and faculty to receive the royalties they deserve.

A searchable, sortable library enables faculty members throughout the institution to share "learning objects" (e.g., a lecture, PowerPoint slide presentation, a graphic chart, etc). By sharing resources, faculty members can decrease their course development time while enriching their curriculum.

The learning object repository should be flexible and robust; with the ability to allow faculty to easily share content on a course level, department level, institutional level, or even globally.

It is likely that three types of libraries would be needed: a faculty library to manage content; an institution-wide library for faculty to share content learning objects; and a global library to share with other institutions and companies if desired. The learning object repository should be flexible and robust; with the ability to allow faculty to easily share content on a course level, department level, institutional level, or even globally. When sharing with organizations outside the institution, it is necessary to have the ability to track usage in order to account for distribution of royalties to staff and/or the institution. This issue is very particularly important for faculty who spend considerable time developing their materials and want to be compensated for their intellectual properties. It also can lead to a revenue stream for institutions that choose to work collaboratively with other institutions or for-profit companies.

■ Six: an integrator to take course content from the virtual world into the administrative world

As I stated earlier, many vendors and institutions have put their focus primarily on course content. For this reason, some faculty members are already accustomed to specific software and are reluctant to learn new applications. For this reason, institutions need the ability to integrate course content data from any or all of their connected learning courses regardless of the content creation product — into its connected learning and their administrative system. This integration enables institutions to manage their total connected learning solutions on an enterprise level while offering faculty members the flexibility of choice they want.

Source: Peggi Munkittrick, "Building a Foundation for Connected Learning," T.H.E. Journal, April 2000. Reprinted with permission of the author.

E-learning Application

Chapter 16

Corporate Universities:
An Interview with Jeanne Meister

By James L. Morrison

Jeanne Meister is president of Corporate University Xchange, Inc., a research and consulting firm that launches corporate universities within Fortune 1000 companies as well as small and medium-sized companies. Corporate University Xchange conducts advanced research on the relationship between business strategy and learning and is a prominent authority on that topic.

James L. Morrison (JLM): *Jeanne, what is a corporate university?*
Jeanne Meister (JM): As we think of it, a corporate university is a portal within a company through which all education takes place. It is an organization's strategic hub for educating employees, customers and suppliers. Corporate universities link an organization's strategies to the learning goals of its audiences.

JLM: *How does a corporate university differ from a corporate training department?*
JM: Training departments tend to be reactionary, fragmented, and decentralized, designed to serve a wide audience with an array of open enrollment programs. A corporate university, on the other hand, pulls together all learning in an organization by managing education as a business project. It has one head — either a dean or a chief learning officer — and clear goals, objectives and long-term strategic plans. It works with both outside universities and training vendors to get the best deals (i.e., contracts on design and/or delivery of training services and other learning programs) on behalf of all of the employees in the organization. A corporate university also shapes corporate culture by fostering leadership, creative thinking and problem solving.

A corporate university provides strategically relevant learning solutions for each job family within a corporation. Strategic is the key word here. A strategic learning organization functions as the umbrella for a company's total education requirements — for all employees and the entire value chain, including customers and suppliers. In a corporate university, employees build individual and organizational competencies, thereby improving the company's overall performance.

JLM: *Do corporate universities give degrees?*
JM: In many cases, they award joint degrees with traditional universities. They are not themselves accredited. For example, the Bank of Montreal offers an MBA degree through a joint program with Dalhousie University. Bell Atlantic Learning Center also offers joint degrees with a consortium of 23 universities in New England. Corporate universities do not want their primary function to be granting degrees; they want to partner with universities to provide customized programs for major job families, usually within their organizations. These customized programs may lead to new degrees based on the training needs of the corporation.

... a corporate university can be the ideal means for companies to provide employees with practical business knowledge, managerial competence, and task-oriented education, all designed to make an organization more competitive.

The corporate university concept, as we see it and "preach" it, is not intended to replace the rigor of a traditional education. Obviously a traditional university can do certain things that a corporate university can never hope to achieve, even in the increasingly market-driven arena of business education. For example, traditional universities foster a broad, integrated frame of reference that draws from a wide, multidisciplinary spectrum; corporate universities, unlike regular universities, are not appropriate for — or even capable of — developing the so-called "Renaissance man" (or person). But a corporate university can be the ideal means for companies to provide employees with practical business knowledge, managerial competence, and task-oriented education, all designed to make an organization more competitive.

JLM: *Could you give us some idea of the breadth, scope and future of corporate universities?*
JM: Our database lists more than 1,600 organizations titled "corporate universities," "corporate colleges," or "institutes for learning." We expect this number to increase to more than 2,000 in the next few years. We believe that by the year 2010 or so, corporate universities will outnumber traditional universities.

As you may be aware, traditional universities are closing at the same time that corporate universities are growing. In the past 13 years, more than 100 universities have closed their doors; we believe that there is a huge market opportunity for other universities — and not just those in danger of closing — to partner with corporations.

JLM: *How could a corporate university partner with a traditional university?*
JM: In some cases, a traditional university can simply offer programs on the site of the corporate university. About half of the 1,600 corporations in our database have physical campuses for their corporate universities. They want to bring university programs within their walls, just as they have brought banks, ATMs and even laundry services on the premises so that their employees never have to leave. These corporate universities want not only courses, but also student services, registration offices, libraries and bookstore facilities inside the corporate walls. Some even want to partner with traditional universities to create whole new degree programs. For example, American Express and Rio Salado Community College have joined to create an associate's degree in customer service. I see opportunities to start small and build in many directions.

JLM: *What are the forces driving the development of corporate universities?*
JM: One force is the obsolescence of knowledge. Jobs now require rapidly changing skill sets, so corporations are realizing that even a Phi Beta Kappa graduate needs a lot of training after being hired. Corporations often want new degree programs or curricula for engineers or manufacturing people, and they become frustrated when universities cannot create these programs quickly. They have begun to take these matters into their own hands by partnering with universities, training vendors, or even publishers, who are becoming more directly involved with education.

JLM: *I've heard you use the expression "Dell or be Delled." You said that this phrase is a wake-up call for American higher education. What did you mean?*
JM: I was referring to a recent article on that topic that appeared in the Wall Street Journal last year. Dell Computer has been enormously successful in bypassing retailers and going directly to consumers with their product, providing excellent customer service. I think the same thing is true for higher education. Companies are going to bypass universities that don't provide what they want, and they are going to go directly to publishers for training materials. This has already started with Harcourt University and Dow Jones University. So higher education has the potential of being "Delled" when corporations go directly to the source of the content that they want taught.

JLM: *So corporations will become competitors with traditional universities?*

JM: Yes. Some corporations are spending a lot of money on higher education. Among the organizations we work with, the average budget for the corporate university is $20 million. In some organizations, this budget reaches $600 million. What is the budget of a four-year land-grant university?

JLM: *What is the funding model of the corporate university?*
JM: The funding model of the corporate university is changing. It used to be that corporations would write a check and say, "Here's the money for the training program." Now, funding training is so expensive that, rather than writing a $10 million check, companies expect corporate universities to be nearly self-funded or even to provide revenue for the parent organization. Corporations now want to set up training programs like a traditional university and charge tuition to their internal business clients. Those clients might be the heads of sales or the heads of manufacturing within the companies. But companies also want to take the materials that they have copyrighted and market them to the customers and suppliers in their networks. They can make money licensing those materials to outsiders for a fee. So the funding model is changing from a cost-center to a fee-for-services, self-funded model.

JLM: *And by implication, when a corporate university develops specific content dealing with services, finance, engineering or human relations, it could then market that content even beyond its own suppliers?*
JM: Yes. If a company spends $10 million on education, that same company may be spending $200 million on advertising in order to build its brand in the marketplace. So companies want to leverage their strong brand positioning and sell education.

JLM: *Many traditional colleges and universities are developing online learning and online courses. Are corporate universities doing the same thing?*
JM: Definitely. Our survey of 120 corporate universities reveals that, in the next three years, almost 60 percent of their coursework will be delivered through the corporate intranet. Employees will register and take modules online and alert their managers to these activities. Both groups can thereby assess skills, compare skills with those required for a given position and choose materials to help close any gaps. The corporate intranet will provide training via courseware, videos and/or audiotapes.

JLM: *Thank you, Jeanne, for giving us your perspective of corporate education and the implications of this phenomenon for higher education.*

Source: James Morrison, "*Corporate Universities: An Interview with Jeanne Meister,*" Technology Source, July/August 2000. *Reprinted with permission of the author.*

Chapter 17
E-learning and Educational Transformation:
An Interview with Greg Priest

BY JAMES L. MORRISON

Greg Priest has served as president and CEO of Smart Force, formerly known as CBT Systems, since December 1998. His previous positions include chief financial officer for SmartForce and president and CEO of Knowledge Well, which was acquired by SmartForce in 1998. Prior to joining SmartForce in 1995, Priest was an attorney with Wilson, Sonsini, Goodrich & Rosati, a Silicon Valley-based law firm that represents emerging growth technology companies.

James Morrison [JM]: *Greg, you are the chief executive officer of SmartForce, a company that provides "learning solutions based on e-learning." What is e-learning?*

Greg Priest [GP]: There is a transformation going on in education. I think that the single most important driver of that transformation is the Internet. Essentially, e-learning is using the special capabilities of the Internet as a delivery method to reinvent the way that people learn.

The Internet has enormous power to improve the educational process. By using the Internet, education can be personalized to each user, so that each student is given a targeted set of materials based on his or her specific educational goals and previous achievements. At the same time, the Internet allows material to be updated dynamically, which creates an up-to-the minute resource for students.

The Internet also allows for collaboration in a way that has not been possible before with technology-based learning — collaboration not only with the student at the next desk, but also with a student half a world away.

Finally, the Internet is interlinked. It is called the "Web" for a reason. The ability to connect different kinds of resources so that they become a coherent whole is an opportunity to create an integrated curriculum out of an incredibly wide range of source material.

The net effect of all of this is that education is becoming increasingly targeted to the individual; it is going to be integrated more completely into our daily lives, generating a process of lifelong learning, and it is going to happen in real time.

JM: *Is it your belief that e-learning will replace professors? If not, how can we assist educators in using technology tools?*
GP: Of course, there are self-styled "visionaries" who present a vision of the future that involves the elimination of all human interaction. That is nonsense. E-learning will never replace faculty, but it may cause faculty to place more emphasis on mentoring and facilitation.

Certainly, some educational goals can be achieved through the use of tecnology-based formats. Ever since the invention of the printing press, people have learned from books. Similarly, people can learn through technology. Books alone are not enough, nor are any of the other technologies by themselves enough.

> *Technology is a tool; by itself it cannot teach anything. The human element is a critical component of the educational process.*

Technology is a tool; by itself it cannot teach anything. The human element is a critical component of the educational process. The key is to create a set of tools that can be used most effectively to leverage the teacher's time and energy, so that the teacher spends the most time doing those things that add the most value to the learning process. This way, faculty can harness the power in these tools for teaching and research.

JM: *We all recognize that lifelong learning is an essential educational goal. How can e-learning help us to achieve it?*
GP: The vision that I have of lifelong learning is a process where individuals are constantly engaged in an exercise of upgrading their skills and abilities. In order to realize that vision, we have to give all individuals exactly the material they want for exactly the purpose they want to achieve at exactly the time they need it. That requires the infrastructure provided by e-learning.

In order to turn that vision into a reality, the infrastructure alone is not enough. The infrastructure needs to be used by educators to offer the substance that people want and need. That work hasn't been completed, but that is where we — as a company, as an industry and as a society — are moving.

JM: *One of the concerns educators have about technology-based instruction is that there is not sufficient instructor-student interaction. How will you address this concern?*

GP: Historically, methods of technology-based instruction have involved a trade-off. In order to get the convenience and cost advantages of technology, you had to give up real, direct interactivity. This was true until recently.

But as I mentioned just a moment ago, one of the powers of the Internet is the degree to which we are able to transcend those limitations today. Using the Internet, a student can ask a question of a faculty member or a teaching assistant anytime or anywhere and often get a real-time response. Individual students can have one-to-one conversations about the course. Groups of students can come together for a live, real-time discussion group related to the course.

Virtually all of the interactions that are possible in a live classroom environment are replicable in the Internet environment. In fact, in some ways, the interactivity is more powerful. Students can interact with other students via threaded interaction even if they cannot be available at precisely the same time. Students can interact with students who are geographically remote. Neither of these is possible in a traditional classroom environment.

> *Virtually all of the interactions that are possible in a live classroom environment are replicable in the Internet environment. In fact, in some ways, the interactivity is more powerful.*

The existing issues do not relate to whether the technology is capable of supporting a high level of interaction. First, vendors must understand how critical it is to enable meaningful interactions within their systems, and second, any teachers who are using systems must learn to foster interaction. These issues require vendors to think differently about what they are building and teachers to think differently about how they teach. Both of those are possible. Both of those will happen. But it is a challenge.

Just as an example of the kind of power the Internet brings, one of the fastest growing parts of SmartForce's business is an online mentoring structure that allows 24/7 access to subject matter experts who mentor students on our Internet-based courseware.

JM: *In closing, if you could make one point to professional educators about e-learning, what would it be?*

GP: E-learning is a tool. It is a very powerful tool, but it is only a tool. Just as Internet "visionaries" who prophesy the elimination of faculty are naîve, those who proclaim that using technology to improve the learning process is a slippery slope, that it will somehow destroy the basic instructor-student model of education, are incorrect.

Technology has created a powerful set of tools for us to use in the educational world. Things like electronic storage and retrieval of text and the personal computer have been powerful forces for the betterment of education and scholarship. In fact, one of the first effective uses of the Internet was as a medium for scholars to communicate among themselves the results of their research.

If used effectively by educators, the Internet and e-learning can improve education and scholarship immeasurably. Educators can have a profoundly positive influence on how the Internet is leveraged to improve education, but they will have to engage with technology in order to do so.

In short, the Internet is such a powerful medium that it is going to change the face of education. Whether that change is for good or ill depends on the talents and motivations of the people implementing it.

Source: James Morrison, "E-learning and Educational Transformation: An Interview with Greg Priest," Technology Source, May/June 2000. Reprinted with permission of the author.

Chapter 18

Conducting a University Human Resource Development Degree Program Through Multiple Technology Delivery Modes:
A Case Study

BY CHRIS ZIRKLE, PH.D.

Colleges and universities across the nation have recently faced several changes impacting the nature of courses and degree programs they offer (Zirkle & Shoemaker, 1999). Many students want to pursue degrees and professional development opportunities without relocating. Legislators and taxpayers have raised the issue of greater accountability and quality in post-secondary education. Traditional colleges and universities are facing increased competition for students from corporate universities and proprietary, for-profit schools. All of these pressures have created some innovative approaches to course delivery methodologies and degree requirements, many which utilize new information technology tools.

Indiana State University (ISU), which has a rich tradition of involvement with technical/technology education, dedicated the John T. Myers Technology Center in October 1998. The building, which houses over 30 specialized laboratories, supports five departments in the School of Technology: aerospace, electronics/ computer technology, industrial/mechanical technology, manufacturing/construction technology, and industrial technology education. The Department of Industrial Technology Education (ITE), which employs six full-time faculty, offers bachelor's and master's degrees in human resource development, technology education, and career and technical education. A new doctoral program, with a specialization area in human resource development and industrial, was added in late 1998. While many of the enrollees in these programs are traditional, full-time students, a growing number are employed professionals seeking new skills and knowledge.

Many of these students are time-bound and place-bound. They are unable to come to campus and participate in a traditional on-campus degree program. Also, while most students reside in Indiana, increasingly students are enrolling from other states, especially in the human resource development (HRD) program.

■ Program and Faculty Structure

The ITE department offers approximately 12 HRD courses per semester; about two-thirds are at the graduate level. For students who prefer an emphasis on face-to-face interaction with peers and professors, all classes are offered on campus (Zirkle & Shoemaker, 1999). But virtually all of the ITE courses each semester are also taught using three alternative simultaneous delivery methods: for students at remote sites who can accommodate live courses into their work schedules, a satellite system is available. For those who work irregular hours from week to week and cannot commit to scheduled classes, videotapes are a viable option. For those who need even more flexibility, an Internet-based instructional program is available for use at home at any hour of the day. Each course delivery option offers its own advantages; for example, students from out-of-state who take the courses on videotape have their out-of-state tuition waived. Students selecting the Internet option can complete an entire master's degree in Human Resource Development through online work. The bachelor's degree in HRD can also be completed at a distance through a combination of on-line, videotape and correspondence courses. Many students experiment with different methods, taking some courses on campus and others via other delivery methods.

Students selecting the Internet option can complete an entire master's degree in Human Resource Development through online work. The bachelor's degree in HRD can also be completed at a distance through a combination of on-line, videotape and correspondence courses.

Each faculty member in the department teaches at least one course each week via multiple delivery (Zirkle & Ourand, 1999). They teach the traditional courses to on-campus students in a specially designed studio while distance students at the various satellite sites participate simultaneously. After each class, videotapes of the session are mailed to those students who have requested that mode of delivery. The instructor then accesses the course Web site and posts lecture notes, presentation slides, audio/video files, and other information that students taking the course via the Internet may need. Some faculty uses Blackboard Inc.'s CourseInfo software to support their Web instruction; others have custom-designed their own course sites.

The ITE department began offering HRD courses in 1990 through the Indiana Higher Education Telecommunication System (IHETS), a state-funded consortium of eight member college and university campuses initiated by the 1967 Indiana General Assembly. This system utilizes digitally compressed satellite technology to reach over 325 sites across the state. IHETS sites include many of Indiana's college campuses, public schools, libraries, hospitals, and other easily accessible facilities. One of the several IHETS studios at Indiana State University serves as the classroom for on-campus students, from which they can interact with students at other IHETS sites as well. This arrangement also allows for videotaping of classes, which are distributed to students at a distance with no access to an IHETS site. In 1997-98, the ITE department added Internet courses. With this, students have the option of taking courses through one of four delivery formats: traditional on-campus delivery, IHETS satellite, videotape, and the Internet. As of the fall of 2000, approximately 20 percent of the students are on-campus, 25 percent are utilizing the IHETS system, 5-10 percent use videotape and the remainder are taking courses on the Internet. The Internet group is the fastest growing (Zirkle & Ourand, 1999).

◼ *Interaction Issues with Multiple Delivery*

The traditional students on campus can meet with professors before and after class meetings and have access to several computer labs to e-mail their instructors, participate in live chat sessions, and complete assignments. For students participating from off campus, faculty supplement e-mail and telephone contact with a variety of other options. IHETS students can communicate with faculty through satellite transmission, which allows for audio communications. Students taking courses via videotape send written reactions to their instructors via mail, fax, or e-mail on a weekly basis. Internet students utilize mailing lists, chat rooms, and discussion boards to communicate with faculty and other students. Faculty have also experimented with online "office hours" where students can log on at specified times and talk with the instructor via an office "chat room." (Zirkle & Shoemaker, 1999). For many, the telephone is still the preferred method of communication.

Delivering courses in a number of different formats can create interaction challenges for both faculty and students. With the exception of on-campus students, a lack-of eye-to-eye contact is an issue for IHETS, videotape and Internet students. Faculty are unable to view student visual reaction to the presentation of material. There are limitations on some types of learning activities. Group, cooperative activities are limited, as are "hands-on", psychomotor activities, especially for Internet students. Student participation can be difficult to monitor for faculty as well. Finally response time is a concern for videotape students. They receive a videotape of the class several days after it is broadcast on IHETS. They have to view the tape and then make any inquiries to the faculty afterward.

■ Assessment Concerns

With students at various "distances", it can be problematic to assess student performance. It is difficult to monitor work ownership, to ensure students are truly doing their own work. The issue of class participation can also be an assessment concern. The level of class participation can be difficult to judge when the student is in a satellite TV studio 150 miles away, or sitting in front of a computer screen. Faculty are also challenged to return student work in a timely fashion, especially when it arrives via regular mail, email, fax or in-person.

To address some of these issues, faculty has arranged to have exams proctored for students at remote sites. Faculty also develop multiple versions of the same exam and distribute them randomly as a way to discourage "community learning" on exams.

■ What About Faculty Training?

Obviously, teaching courses through multiple delivery formats requires a high level of expertise on the part of the faculty (Zirkle & Ourand, 1999). Faculty development is a top concern. Most need familiarization with the university computer network, which is a mixed Novell and UNIX environment. The ability to create web pages and Internet courses is a necessity. Perhaps most important is the ability to transfer traditional, standard course material to the satellite system and the Internet. These needs, along with others, have created numerous professional development challenges for faculty.

Many faculty in the ITE department have participated in training sessions to learn how to utilize the various technologies that support multiple delivery platforms. Indiana State University sponsors the Course Transformation Academy (CTA), a development program designed to give faculty members the time and resources they need to investigate, create, and utilize alternative instructional strategies (Zirkle & Shoemaker, 1999). The CTA offers semester-long workshops for groups of 15-20 faculty members, as well as an intensive, one-week summer workshop. Participants use hands-on projects to learn about creating Web-based, broadcast, and interactive video courses and about incorporating supplementary technologies — such as videotapes and audio-conferencing — into their instruction. As they work with the technologies, faculty members use asynchronous and synchronous tools to discuss pedagogical issues, course design considerations and assessment

As they work with the technologies, faculty members use asynchronous and synchronous tools to discuss pedagogical issues, course design considerations and assessment strategies.

strategies. They receive information about three important subjects: the University's policies on intellectual property and copyright fair use, its distance education student services, and University resources available to assist faculty members in course development and delivery. During the CTA, participants have opportunities to work on aspects of their own courses as they complete projects designed to enhance their technological competencies.

Indiana State University also has a Faculty Computing Resource Center (FCRC) designed to provide faculty with one-on-one consultations and conduct workshops and demonstrations on a wide range of topics, such as web page construction, video and audio streaming, and graphics development. Full-time technical experts staff the FCRC, but part-time student workers, who are in many cases very familiar with specific software applications, web page development, and audio or video manipulation, give much of the assistance provided to faculty.

Much faculty learning is "on-the-job" and from each other. Faculty share experiences and ideas, along with new discoveries, many made by trial-and-error, as they work with the multiple delivery format.

■ Other Issues

There are additional concerns for faculty, not the least of which is the time constraint that is imposed from the multiple delivery modes. While the maximum number of students in an ITE course is generally capped at 40, the number of distance students can easily be 75 percent of that total. This results in a significant number of e-mails, phone calls and other requests for information from distance students that do not have immediate classroom access to the instructor. Faculty are given the equivalent of a two-course "load" for each multiple delivery format course they teach (Zirkle & Ourand, 1999).

While technology has certainly allowed the department to deliver the courses, it is not foolproof.

While technology has certainly allowed the department to deliver the courses, it is not foolproof. Students have periodic problems with the satellite transmission, and many experience difficulties with accessing course sites on the Internet and performing such tasks as live chat or on-line office hours. While the university has established a toll-free technical support line and has increased student services for distance students, the course instructor is still the first contact for many concerns. This creates yet another time constraint for faculty.

The ITE department is also concerned with issues of quality and consistency. Are all four groups receiving the same level of instruction? Is there enough interaction for distance students? Do on-campus students get the same exposure to technology that distance students receive? These issues are discussed are discussed on a frequent basis by ITE faculty.

■ Curricular Benefits

The multiple delivery formats have produced several positive benefits for students and faculty. The department has experienced increased enrollment; most classes offered by the multiple delivery format in the 1999-2000 school year were closed due to high enrollment. The student demographic has also changed. Because of the increased ease of access, more nontraditional students have enrolled. Additionally, at the undergraduate level, a partnership between Indiana State University and Indiana's Technical Colleges (IVY TECH), called DegreeLink, has allowed students to earn postsecondary degrees through a set of "2+2" articulation agreements. Students who earn an associate's degree at IVY TECH can transfer their earned course credit to Indiana State University, and then enter ISU with junior-year status. The HRD bachelor's degree program is a DegreeLink program.

Faculty, despite the increased workload, see the multiple delivery format as a professional growth opportunity. It has required them to keep current with the latest instructional technologies and computer hardware/software changes, which has tremendous implications for HRD professionals. It has also allowed them to "extend their sphere of influence" from beyond the traditional campus. The department now has students from more than a dozen states. The faculty believes it has helped strengthen both the content of, and discussion in, classes.

The multiple delivery format is firmly established in the department. All faculty are expected to deliver courses in this manner. It has enabled the department to deliver courses to meet the specific learning needs of their students, no matter where they are located. This outreach has allowed the department to remain competitive and accountable in today's postsecondary marketplace.

■ References

Zirkle, C. & D. Ourand, D., *Teaching a Course Through Multiple Delivery Systems: Some Lessons Learned.* ERIC Document Reproduction Service No. 435, 1999, p. 800.

Zirkle, C. & H. Shoemaker, "Indiana State's Multiple Delivery Approach: Integrating Industrial Technology Education with Educational Technology." *The Technology Source* 1999, November-December, [Online]. Available: http://horizon.unc.edu/Ts/cases/1999-11.asp

Chapter 19
The Catalyst Project:
Supporting Faculty Uses of the Web...with the Web

BY MARK DONOVAN AND SCOTT MACKLIN

Since 1994, UWired, a collaborative unit at the University of Washington, has worked to develop and improve ways to support faculty teaching with new technologies. In 1998, UWired initiated a series of activities aimed at reinventing its support structure and redefining the role of the university's Center for Teaching, Learning, and Technology. In early 1999, UWired launched the Catalyst project, the most visible manifestation of its new approach. This chapter details the strategic plan behind the Catalyst project and the redefinition of the center.

Finding ways to effectively support teaching with new technologies has been a vexing problem for colleges and universities. A variety of strategies have been advocated for engaging faculty and providing faculty support and training, and many articles on the topic published in practitioner journals include laundry lists of strategies to motivate, incent, train, and otherwise cajole faculty into integrating technology into their teaching.

It is clear that institutional contexts and culture, not to mention the underlying technological infrastructure, have a profound influence on the effectiveness of faculty support and development strategies. It is also clear that there are real barriers to faculty adoption of instructional technology, including concerns about intellectual property, the disconnect between innovation in teaching and tenure decisions and disciplinary rewards, and the preeminence of research activity at some institutions. In addition, there is a segment of the faculty (a diminishing minority, we will argue) that is uninterested and even hostile to technology.

The difficulties inherent in promoting and supporting good instructional uses of technology can be paralyzing. Yet the risk is not so much that faculty support staff will be paralyzed, but rather that we will become so attuned to our current difficulties that we will fail to understand fully the transformative effect of the technologies we promote and support, and thus will be left trying hard to solve yesterday's problem.

In the earlier years of the Web, say 12 to 36 months ago, many campuses responded to the challenges of instructional technology support by establishing campus centers for teaching, learning, and technology. These centers typically host workshops and training, organize recurring "show and tell" conferences, provide one-on-one consulting with educational technologists and instructional designers, convene faculty "brown bag" sessions, and often initiate mini-grant competitions designed to provide extended (often expensive) support for particular faculty projects. These centers typically work with a small percentage of highly motivated faculty.

The problem in motivating faculty to learn about new teaching methods is difficult regardless of whether or not technology is involved. . . .

But what about the rest? In conversations with colleagues, we have heard those faculty members who don't participate in such activities labeled "disinterested," "hard to reach," "resistant," and — the put-down of last resort — "luddites." In a recent article entitled "'Where Are They?': Why Technology Education for Teachers Can Be So Difficult," Claudia Rebaza laments the declining turnout at her institution's instructional technology conferences.[1] She ultimately concludes:

> The problem in motivating faculty to learn about new teaching methods is difficult regardless of whether or not technology is involved. . . . No matter how many learning opportunities you offer— lectures, hands-on workshops, handouts, classes, computer tutorials, media guides—what people really will find most helpful is a one-on-one approach, with instruction at the point of need. As demand for "convenience learning" continues to grow, it may be that competitive pressures and a healthy respect for the bottom line will achieve the faculty cooperation no other motivation can bring.

We think she gets this equation half right — and backwards. "Instruction at the point of need" is a crucial concept. Will institutional demands to provide "convenience learning" result in faculty being forced to adopt technology? Perhaps. But it could also be that the increasing ubiquity of networked information technologies will result in faculty themselves seeking out convenient, just-in-time learning to support their efforts to use technology.

This, we think, is a crucial point: While early adopters sought out personal assistance and allies to support them in what have often been contrarian activities, we believe the next wave of faculty adopters will be more interested in finding support and assistance via the Web. UWired has worked over the past year and half to turn this hypothesis into a robust program for faculty support.

■ UWired

In 1994, the University of Washington established UWired as a collaborative unit designed to find, develop, promote, and support effective uses of teaching and learning with technology. From the outset, UWired has played an important coordinating role, bringing the collective expertise of its five partners —Computing & Communications, University Libraries, the Office of Undergraduate Education, the Office of Educational Partnerships, and Educational Outreach — to bear on common challenges and opportunities posed by the academic uses of information technology.

UWired is involved in supporting up to a dozen programs or initiatives aimed at promoting technology access, information literacy and fluency, with information technology and technology-based innovation in teaching.

With a staff of between five and seven full-time professionals and upwards of 75 students, UWired has functioned as a lean and flexible organization that has primary responsibility for the university's central student computing labs (325 seats) and faculty technology support. In addition, at any given time UWired is involved in supporting up to a dozen programs or initiatives aimed at promoting technology access, information literacy and fluency, with information technology and technology-based innovation in teaching.

The actual capacity and reach of UWired are dependent on the close working relationship developed among the UWired partners and other campus affiliates (such as the Office of Educational Assessment, the College of Arts & Sciences, and the School of Library and Information Science). This collaborative approach reduces the duplication of effort and resources, speeds the identification of new challenges and opportunities, and improves communication between units at a very large and highly distributed university. The importance of this collaboration was never more evident than when UWired began a fundamental rethinking of its faculty support model a little over 18 months ago.

■ Rethinking faculty support

In 1996, UWired established the Center for Teaching, Learning and Technology to provide front-line support for faculty who wished to experiment with new technologies, not unlike the centers established at other institutions. Workshops, drop-in consulting, and intensive, project-based support were provided free of charge to faculty who sought out assistance. Midway through 1998 we projected 1,700 annual visits to the center, more than double those of the preceding year. Based on that statistic, it seemed that we were doing our job, but a look below the surface suggested that we were not having the impact — or playing the role — that best suited our position.

As faculty use of technology becomes the norm, we find the pragmatists far more interested in finding just-in-time support than in finding like-minded supporters.

The majority of the visits to our center were from teaching assistants and "the usual suspects" — faculty with whom UWired had established a relationship, often on the basis of a project we supported under a mini-grant initiative. While the use of our facility was on the increase, we saw no evidence that the reach of our support had likewise been extended. We found ourselves grappling with a question common these days to those in faculty support roles — how to reach beyond the early adopters? By talking with faculty, meeting with college and department heads, and conducting faculty focus groups, we began to understand that, as technology use spread beyond the early adopters to the pragmatists who largely composed the university community, our strategy for supporting faculty would also have to change.

The early adopters who sought out our center were willing to make the trek across campus from their office and often seemed in search of allies as much as they were in search of technical assistance. As faculty use of technology becomes the norm, we find the pragmatists far more interested in finding just-in-time support than in finding like-minded supporters. Furthermore, our vision of the center as a place where faculty could drop in and work required that we configure the center like a drop-in lab with each workstation configured with a standard set of tools. As Web technologies have become more diverse and complex, this need to provide standard tools conflicted with the need to experiment with hardware and software and the diverse technology solutions that were taking hold in various colleges and departments.

■ *Faculty support in a multi-tiered system*

As we rethought our role in supporting faculty uses of instructional technology, we found ourselves pinched between the needs of faculty to make use of the centrally supported university IT infrastructure and the particularities of their college or departmental environment. This tension hinted at the direction of our reinvention — we needed to translate the central infrastructure and find ways to provide common support that did not conflict with the idiosyncrasies of the local computing environment. As we discuss in detail, providing educationally focused, flexible support via the Web became the cornerstone of our strategy.

The foundation for instructional technology at the University of Washington is the vast, robust network infrastructure developed and maintained by Computing & Communications (C&C). The heavily used network involves ubiquitous Ethernet connectivity and transfers an average of more than one million e-mail messages and 700 gigabytes of data each day. C&C hosts more than 70,000 user accounts and nearly 18,000 Web sites for individuals and organizations on campus. C&C's enterprise computing model is centered on providing a standards-based infrastructure that allows units within the university to build and deploy the kinds of applications that fit their specific needs.

Because of this multi-tiered architecture, the local computing environment of the faculty varies greatly owing to different needs, cultures and decision-making processes at the college and department level. For example, some col-

> *Because of this multi-tiered architecture, the local computing environment of the faculty varies greatly owing to different needs, cultures and decision-making processes at the college and department level.*

leges and departments have adopted standard Web authoring tools (such as Macromedia's Dreamweaver or Microsoft's FrontPage) while others have implemented courseware solutions (such as WebCT or Blackboard's CourseInfo). Rather than try to promote a campus standard for such tools, we recognized that differences in unit needs and capacity were driving this diversity. Furthermore, we believed that there was a great potential that this diversity of approaches would lead to accelerated experimentation, innovation, and learning about the effective uses of technology in teaching.

Our appreciation for the diversity of college and departmental needs also led to encounters with those staff members responsible for supporting faculty uses of technology within academic departments. We discovered a general ambivalence to the existence of UWired and the Center for Teaching, Learning, and Technology and found it was seen as a place where some faculty went to receive help. For the most part, our activities did nothing to add value to the work of these departmental staffers since we typically worked with the eager early adopters, and the department staff were often left working with those pragmatic faculty who, while interested in using technology, were not interested in straying too far from their office to learn.

Our strategy was also based on a belief that the penetration of information technology is changing faculty work habits and expectations in ways that are not yet being fully appreciated.

Departmental technology staff are a diverse lot, running the gamut from trained technologists to graduate students working for a stipend. Many are staff members hired for another role who, by virtue of their technical skills and ability to work with faculty, end up supporting technology at the desktop, replacing hard drives, and assisting faculty with course Web pages. Many of these departmental support staff spends considerable energies developing materials to tutor faculty on instructional uses of technology. In rare cases they were also assisting faculty in the creation of Web-based instructional software. It was clear to us that there was an excellent opportunity for UWired to invent an effort which would bridge the gap between a world-class network infrastructure and the academic departments where the bulk of the instructional work was being done.

Our strategy was also based on a belief that the penetration of information technology is changing faculty work habits and expectations in ways that are not yet being fully appreciated. It is common for those of us supporting academic computing to argue at once that networked technologies drive individual and social change, yet faculty are somehow inoculated from these changes and will not get up to speed with technology without our intervention and assistance and a healthy (though rarely forthcoming) set of rewards and incentives. This argument for "academic exceptionalism" — one we have at times promoted —ignores the ways that network technologies pervade the lives of faculty in their roles as citizen, researcher, and hobbyist. While it is true that there is much work to be done to couple innovation in teaching with the rewards of the tenure system, we believe that this articulation will follow, not precede, the diffusion of technology in teaching. In Washington, a state in which the software industry holds the largest payroll and which boasts the third largest percentage of home computer ownership and households online, our intuition was that information technologies, specifically e-mail and the Web, were already becoming deeply ingrained in the life of our faculty.

Through our partnership with the University Libraries, UWired included measures of faculty technology use in the Libraries' 1998 triennial user survey.[2] What we found confirmed our intuition and helped to clarify our strategy. Of the faculty surveyed (N = 1,503), 84% responded that the Web was very important for their work, 91% reported using e-mail to communicate with students, and 31% reported putting course material (beyond a simple syllabus) on the Web. The picture that emerged from this survey was of a faculty already deeply committed to using the technologies we were working to support. As we thought about how to reposition UWired's faculty support efforts to fulfill the role of translator and coordinator of information about technology in teaching and learning, it became clear to us that the challenge was that of supporting instructional uses of technology through these same technologies.

■ *The Catalyst project*

The Catalyst project, which emerged from this period of examination and reflection, is based on the following assumptions:

➤ faculty want just-in-time learning and support,

➤ they prefer to do this learning at their own pace, in their local environment,

➤ the Web is or will become the vehicle of choice for just-in-time information and learning,

➤ distributed support personnel are best suited to make the critical decisions about local infrastructure and local support, and

➤ the key function for UWired — the value add — is in capturing, focusing, and disseminating the ideas, resources, and tools that allow both faculty members and local support personnel to make innovative use of new technologies in teaching and learning with a minimum of duplicative effort.

While distributing FAQs and how-to materials via the Web is a standard practice of academic computing groups, there is a significant difference between simply posting information and creating a comfortable, useful Web-based environment that meets the needs of a diverse set of faculty. We sought to create an easily navigable clearinghouse for information on the use of the Web in teaching and learning and also hoped that the site would become a catch basin for the many scattered but impressive technology efforts on campus. By creating a site that would meet faculty needs and draw repeat visits, we hoped to create a center of gravity for innovation in teaching with technology that would far exceed the reach of our physical Center for Teaching, Learning and Technology.

We have previously described in detail the development of the Catalyst site.[3] The site consists of four basic types of content:

1. *Profiles* of educators and programs that provide a vehicle to share ideas and experience, humanize the use of technology, and hopefully diffuse innovations.

2. *Guides* to instructional methods and technology tasks that present material in a familiar framework and provide a map to a wide range of individual documents.

3. *Dynamic content* providing frequently updated information on news and events relevant to teaching with technology.

4. *Instructional tools* that provide a standard mechanism for faculty to create interactive, Web-based instructional modules using only a Web browser. Because we do not distribute software, our model is actually that of providing a Web-based service.

We were determined at the outset to create a Web property that would be immediately useful and intuitive to navigate. We understood that attempts to provide "good information" would fall flat if end users were unable to find the information they needed or otherwise experienced frustration with the site. Key to achieving this goal was the work of our information designer who created a clean, intuitive look and feel for the site, an aspect of Catalyst that has been widely praised by faculty.

The site is built on a simple, tested architecture that relies on a limited number of icons, a clear color scheme to categorize content, and a standard page layout that makes it easy for users to navigate and quickly scan for useful information. The site relies on small graphical elements that speed viewing over a slow connection, and the pages of the site have been designed to easily print out for those who prefer reading from paper rather than the screen. Our how-to guides (Quick Guides) are each centered on a particular task and map each task on a standard four-part framework:

Plan > Create > Connect > Reflect.

In addition to creating a helpful resource, we wanted to create something that would in a sense become "public property," by encouraging others outside of UWired to contribute to its development. To facilitate this, we consciously attempted to create a new brand identity for the university's educational technology efforts. We deemed this important for three reasons. First, a new, identifiable brand focuses educators on a single, stable source of information and resources, providing new opportunities to coordinate information and resources and creating the critical mass for ideas that might otherwise be overlooked. Second, the new identity creates a sense of newness and opportunity, "wiping the slate clean" of previous, perhaps negative, associations of technology and technology support. Finally, the new brand creates opportunities for partnerships and collaboration by emphasizing UWired's coordinating role while de-emphasizing any (false) sense that UWired controlled these activities.

Our desire to use Catalyst to leverage the work of others is just picking up steam, but our initial experience has been encouraging. Departments and college support personnel who have developed materials specific to their local computing environments — e.g., how-to documents on a particular Web editor — have been eager to see their work repackaged and made available to a much larger audience. While we generally favor off-the-shelf solutions over homegrown ones, our Web service model allows us to make specialized Web-based instructional tools widely available. When we identify promising "one off" efforts developed by faculty, we are able to work with these faculty to redesign their tools so that they are secure, scalable and available to the campus community as a Web-based service.

■ A new role for the Center for Teaching, Learning and Technology

To develop and launch Catalyst on a shoestring, we had to commit our staff resources at the Center for Teaching, Learning, and Technology to the development of Web content. As we did this, we began to understand that the continued evolution and improvement of Catalyst would require a reorganization of our staff and the activities of the center to support this effort. This realization necessitated some hard choices. It meant de-emphasizing the primacy of our self-perceived role of providing in-person support to the faculty while having faith that our greatest impact lay in providing timely and accurate information to the faculty we never saw, those who used Catalyst at their desktop. We also curtailed our workshop schedule and focused on preparing workshop materials that, like the other components of Catalyst, could be distributed and used by others.

Figure 1 documents the changes in the organization and operation of the Center for Teaching, Learning and Technology that were initiated to support the

Figure 1. Reorganizing the UWired Center.

OLD	NEW
Drop-in center where faculty could work and receive one-to-one assistance.	Research, development, and demonstration center where Catalyst tools and content are developed and where faculty can drop in and experiment with a range of technology solutions.
Standard software and hardware to provide a uniform and familiar environment for frequent clients.	Highly variegated computing environment where faculty can find a configuration that matches their office environment or test new tools.
Custom solutions tailored to faculty needs, often requiring significant staff time and creating the expectationof continued, intensive support.	Common solutions that address the most frequently expressed needs, customizable by the faculty themselves.
Intensive support for the relatively few physical clients.	Baseline support for many virtual clients.
Frequent drop-in workshops.	Fewer general access workshops, more department-specific workshops.
People-centered service aimed at making clients comfortable using the center.	People-centered service aimed at empowering clients to use technology wherever they are most comfortable.

Catalyst project. In many cases the changes have been invisible to our clients — they still receive the one-to-one assistance many request, but our orientation has shifted away from viewing this as the activity with the largest impact. In fact, as we transitioned into becoming "an RD&D space" (research, development, and demonstration), the energy of our operations increased markedly, and our clients have responded positively. Though a few have complained about the increased noise and activity in our relatively small space (a medium-sized common room with 14 computers, scanners, and printers and two connected offices for developers and consultants), others have clearly enjoyed working in a frenetic, often exciting, environment. Our clients understand that our work is oriented completely around serving faculty, and the fact that this work is visible and not hidden in a back room seems to stimulate their interest and support. On more than one occasion faculty clients have been brought in and contributed to the "whiteboard sessions" that are a frequent part of our operations. While we initially had concerns about how our existing clients would view this reorientation, these were largely unfounded.

The result is that the staff quickly becomes fluent with the technologies we need to support, and as a result of their daily work they often suggest improvements that are ultimately incorporated into technologies made available to our clients.

The ongoing development of Catalyst has been made possible by organizing our staff into content teams that work on different components of the site. These teams, comprised of graduate assistants and undergraduate student staff, work within an established development process and make use of a project-tracking database to facilitate the coordination and handoff of projects among staff who work almost exclusively part-time. The Catalyst team uses the technologies we support to do their work, using for example, off-the-shelf Web products to develop new content and using our Web-based peer review tool to critique and edit proposed content and design changes. The result is that the staff quickly becomes fluent with the technologies we need to support, and as a result of their daily work they often suggest improvements that are ultimately incorporated into technologies made available to our clients.

Our development activity has shifted from a focus on highly customized, boutique solutions that met the need of particular educators — but did not scale — to the development of a modular Web-based suite of services that meet common needs identified through discussions with a wide range of educators. For example, the peer review tool mentioned above was developed in close coordination with campus writing labs. Because it addressed a widely shared need and could be tailored to a specific instructional practice, we thought it warranted the expense of creating a tool (again, really a service) that would be available to the campus at large with accompanying how-to documentation and suggestions for its instructional use. Fundamentally, our goal has shifted from trying to meet the idiosyncratic needs of the individual educator to that of attempting to meet enterprise-wide educational needs.

■ Feedback loops and ongoing development

The Catalyst site was launched in February 1999, and the reception both on campus and off has been better than we hoped.[4] Hundreds of educators have made use of the site and in the first six months of operation —which was purposely marked by little more publicity than a flyer sent to all faculty — our Web tools have been implemented nearly 1,400 times by faculty creating materials for their students.[5] The site has been used by faculty from Anesthesiology to Urban Horticulture (we need to work on the folks in Zoology) at each of three campuses of the University of Washington.

We understand, though, that many a Web site has made an initial splash only to be quickly relegated to memory or an unused browser bookmark. Working from the standpoint that people use the Web with tasks and goals in mind, we have paid considerable attention to user feedback and usability testing and are continually working to improve the design of the site and its offerings. Through a partnership with the Department of Technical Communications, we initiated usability testing immediately after the site launched.[6] We found several areas in need of improvement and immediately went to work to address them. The Catalyst Web site you will find today is thus significantly different from the one that existed just a few months ago. This first round of changes — we anticipate that the site will continually change — included:

➤ adding search functionality,

➤ giving access to the search engine and glossary directly from the standard navigation bar,

➤ eliminating the drop-down menus which were the primary form of site navigation (experienced users liked these, but novice users were confused), and

➤ adding contextual rollovers to orient users better to the Catalyst content categories.

The formal usability test was not our only means of soliciting feedback. We placed feedback forms throughout the Web site and conducted impromptu needs assessment with educators as they utilized the resources of the Center for Teaching, Learning and Technology. In addition, we implemented Web cookies and mechanisms to compile site statistics to help us gather more information about our users and their usage patterns of Catalyst. We intended to use these data to improve the site navigation and the placement and promotion of information that is popular and information that we know to be useful but that users may have a difficult time noticing.

Our goal was not just to create a helpful set of resources, but also to create a site that would draw repeat visits and over time would be viewed as the first place campus educators would look for information about teaching with technology. In the parlance of e-commerce, we wanted to make the site "sticky." Our original design was so focused on making the site useful that we neglected to make the site timely. The current, redesigned site includes four categories of dynamic content which change often and are intended to make Catalyst a site that educators visit frequently:

1. *News & Reviews* contains announcements and reports from conferences, software reviews, and articles about technology on the horizon.

2. *Tips & Tricks* contains technical shortcuts, mini how-to documents, resources for hands-on work, e.g., printing frames, pointer to Adobe's free online tutorials, changing image size for printing in PhotoShop, or creating a table of contents in Microsoft Word.

3. *Events* contains an ongoing calendar of events about teaching with technology.

4. *What's New* on Catalyst provides an opportunity to highlight recent additions to the Catalyst Web site.

> *In the parlance of e-commerce, we wanted to make the site "sticky." Our original design was so focused on making the site useful that we neglected to make the site timely.*

The addition of this dynamic content makes Catalyst more than a (seemingly) static collection of information and provides a vehicle for UWired and others to disseminate information and opinions quickly to the community of educators that we serve. In addition to these changes, our development queue contains several new Web services that meet commonly expressed demands and instructional challenges, including a small-group learning environment tool based on a successful "virtual clinic" experiment in the School of Medicine with broad applications for problem-based learning. Like our other development projects, this tool is being developed in conjunction with educators and assessment experts and upon release will be accompanied by a suite of instructional and technical documentation.

■ Concluding thoughts

Like all of UWired's activities, we view Catalyst as an evolving experiment. Our overarching goal is to create a useful and positive user experience that will translate into innovative uses of technology in teaching and learning.[7] The rapidity of technological (and social) change being wrought by new information technologies has prompted us to look outside the university for insight on how best to organize our operations and develop a Web property that provides leading edge services and support for educators. We have tried to mirror the best practices of Web companies by moving quickly and remaining flexible and responsive in the face of changing needs and opportunities.

Our belief that faculty will increasingly look to the Web for the support they need prompted a fundamental reorganization of our operations that so far appears to be paying off. In just over six months we have completed both the initial launch of the site and significant redesign and have found the reach and impact of this virtual center for teaching, learning, and technology to have exceeded that of our three-year-old physical center. We are connecting with the pragmatists who represent the majority of faculty and not just the early adopters in search of allies.

We recognize that this strategy may not be universally applicable. Catalyst makes sense as a support strategy at our university largely because of the very high penetration of networked technologies, the robust networking infrastructure, and distributed support systems that were already in place, though not yet well connected with each other. Institutions considering a similar strategy would do well to consider these factors in light of their own context and might consider a Catalyst-like set of resources and services to be a second-generation strategy. Having said that, the speed at which the Web and other networked technologies have entered our lives suggests that institutions should think hard about how best to allocate central support resources. The risk in focusing too much on existing support models is that institutions may not be well positioned to address coming challenges.

Source: Mark Donovan and Scott Macklin, "The Catalyst Project: Supporting Faculty Uses of the Web...with the Web," CAUSE/EFFECT Journal, Volume 22, Number 3, 1999. Reprinted with permission of the authors.

◾ Endnotes

1 Claudia Rebaza, "'Where Are They?': Why Technology Education for Teachers Can Be So Difficult," *Technology Source*, June 1998 [http://horizon.unc.edu/TS/vision/1998-06.asp].

2 See http://www.lib.washington.edu/surveys/ for the 1998 survey data and for presentations on this project presented by Lizabeth Wilson, associate director of UW Libraries, and Steve Hiller, head of Science Libraries, for the April 1999 ACRL pre-conference seminar, "Assessing the Academic Networked Environment."

3 See our CAUSE98 paper, "One Size Doesn't Fit All: Designing Scaleable, Client-Centered Support for Technology in Teaching" at http://www.educause.edu/ir/library/html/cnc9846/cnc9846.html, or the condensed version presented as "Supporting Technology in Teaching and Learning: One Size Doesn't Fit All," *Planning for Higher Education*, Fall 1999.

4 The site is viewable to the world at http://depts.washington.edu/catalyst/home.html. Currently the Web services are restricted to members of the University of Washington community.

5 Taking a cue from the restaurant industry, we planned for a "soft launch" of the site in order to ensure that our organizational capacity could keep up with what we hoped would be interest in the site. It did, but just barely, and much of the past summer was taken up with improving operations and making arrangements to ensure that we can handle the feedback and support demands that we expect with the publicity blitz planned for the next academic year.

6 While we had done extensive informal testing of the site architecture, design, and content prior to the public launch that had a dramatic influence on the site, we were unable to complete formal usability testing and meet our launch deadline. When working "on Internet time," there is a very real tension been "good enough" and "just right."

7 We think and talk in terms of promoting "innovation in teaching and learning" rather than "integrating technology in teaching." The usefulness of this perspective is discussed in Mark Donovan, "Rethinking Faculty Support," *Technology Source*, September/October 1999 [http://horizon.unc.edu/TS/development/1999-09.asp].

E-learning Issues

Chapter 20

ROI:
How to do it,
how to prove it

By John Martin

This chapter explores the challenges of quantifying return on investment (ROI) for corporate training and learning. It provides tips for quantifying ROI, case studies of organizations that are examining ROI and a sample ROI calculation.

Roi. In French it means king. In the business world, ROI means return on investment, a signal that an initiative is eminently justifiable. In the world of training, the term means both: ROI is indeed king, and proving it means corporate learning can survive another day.

Strictly speaking, ROI is a percentage derived from the benefits of a particular program (dollars made or saved) divided by its cost. If a $100,000 corporate learning program results in $1 million in additional profit, it could be said to have a return on investment of 1,000 percent.

Strong ROI implies a corporate learning program is tied tightly to overall business goals and not to ivory tower irrelevance. An ROI analysis can spare corporate learning from the budget-cutting ax, unshackle funding for progressive, cutting-edge programs, and in the best case prove that corporate learning is an essential corporate division and can have a positive impact on the bottom line.

Microsoft has even used ROI as a public relations tool: The company trumpeted a whopping 1,800-percent return on investment that it delivered for Hewlett-Packard Company, which last year selected Microsoft's Windows Media streaming technology as the cornerstone for some of its global marketing communications. From a $60,000 investment, HP saved $1.2 million in direct costs the first year as compared to other communications options, according to Microsoft.

Surprisingly, only 14 percent of organizations ever quantify their return on investment, according to a December 1998 survey by the American Management Association (AMA) International. As a result, the vast majority of corporate learning is an act of faith: Competitive companies have well-trained workers, so training must be good. The truth is, sometimes training is good and sometimes it isn't. Sometimes a training program would be good if it were only delivered in a different place, time or by a different method. Too often, however, training is off the mark.

Traditional training groups waste large amounts of money and time, and they're often not in tune with business issues. They need to figure out what's going on in the rest of the organization. And they need to move at the speed of business. They no longer have the luxury of the two-year training rollout.

■ ROI is hard to nail down

While there is a definite need for ROI, calculating it is difficult. Why is ROI so hard to quantify? For one thing, it's extremely difficult to isolate benefits that result from corporate learning programs. If a company's sales force brings in 25 percent more revenue in the 12 months following a sales training program, who's to say that the revenue didn't result from skillful management, a restructuring of incentives, strategic hiring and firing, marketplace shifts, or just good salespeople?

Another reason ROI is hard to quantify is that it's challenging to develop a big picture view of corporate learning, its costs and its benefits.

Another reason ROI is hard to quantify is that it's challenging to develop a big picture view of corporate learning, its costs and its benefits. Several departments might be responsible for managing the necessary data for an ROI calculation, forcing managers to spend too much time tracking it down and sewing it together. Like it or not, however, any solid ROI calculation will start with the small picture — quantifiable variables like tuitions, licenses and numbers of extra widgets sold after training.

Yet another reason ROI is difficult to quantify is that it runs counter to traditional methods of evaluation. Often used, but deservedly maligned, smile sheets are virtually irrelevant to ROI. If they measure anything at all, it's whether the trainers created an effective course — effective, that is, in employees' subjective judgement. Smile sheets say nothing about whether the learning objectives were good for the business. A manager who just got a new multimedia PC might never use PowerPoint, so why should she spend half a day in class learning it as part of computer skills training? Does it matter that she gave the instructor straight A's on the smile sheet?

Other traditional training evaluation methods — pre- and post-assessment and testing to see if employees can transfer their learning to the job — have the same problem: they still presume the learning was necessary and potentially beneficial to the business in the first place.

"The primary evaluation measure for any training program must be: will it help you improve your job performance and the company's business results?" writes Daniel R. Tobin in the Knowledge-Enabled Organization. "Unless employees can return to their jobs and immediately start applying the content of the training to make a noticeable and positive difference in solving business problems and meeting competitive challenges head on, then a training program is indeed a luxury that few companies can afford."

■ Three approaches to quantifying ROI

Ninety-five percent of respondents in the 1998 AMA survey said they measure training effectiveness, but only 14 percent measure ROI. "(And) no two people do it the same way, which is a big reason why some companies that used to conduct such an analysis no longer do one," Eric Rolfe Greenberg, now the AMA's director of management studies, said in a news release.

It is possible to quantify ROI without conducting a formal analysis. Here is how three organizations strove to quantify ROI for their online learning projects.

➤ GenAm Benefits

From the mid-1980s through 1998, GenAm Benefits, now a subsidiary of Great West Life & Annuity Insurance Co., used mainframe computers to train and retrain its 1,000 health, dental and hospital claims professionals in Atlanta, GA., Dallas, TX, Columbus, OH, Rockford, IL., St. Louis and Kennet, MO.

In the late 1990s, the company realized that claims processors would retain more material more quickly through multimedia learning instead of through the mainframe's monochrome text interface. In 1999, GenAm Benefits transformed 85 of its mainframe-based courses into multimedia courses featuring sound, graphics, animation and video. Courses included company fundamentals, data entry, medical terminology, claims processing and coordination of benefits.

GenAm Benefits determined up front that the migration to multimedia learning would cost an extra $25,368 the first year and would save them $36,535 over the next three (1999-2001), mostly in mainframe maintenance and support costs. To come up with these numbers, GenAm Benefits figured the cost of mainframe maintenance, Windows maintenance, mainframe support, licenses, author salaries, author training and a tool that expedites migration. The key is that Windows maintenance costs a fraction of mainframe upkeep.

"Our new multimedia learning just magnifies those benefits, since motivated learners are turning into more proficient producers."

"Our e-learning program helps us avoid the cost of instructor-led learning, keeps employees on the job instead of traveling to a classroom, gives them a ready reference source, and automatically manages registrations, testing, scores and productivity," said Computer-Based Trainer Karen R. Belk. "Our new multimedia learning just magnifies those benefits, since motivated learners are turning into more proficient producers."

But how, specifically, has the learning affected GenAm Benefits' performance? The company hasn't examined the results, at least not in the past couple of years. "The learning that we have conducted has been successful, so management hasn't questioned it," Belk said. "With all the changes in our company, they haven't had time to question it."

➤ The State of Tennessee's Office for Information Resources (OIR)

OIR supports learning needs of 15,000 end users and 1,200 technical people. Although OIR doesn't do formal ROI analysis for training, anyone will tell you that they most certainly manage by data and operate like a business. Every government department says that, but this one actually lives it. OIR gets zero appropriations and instead must earn expenditures from charge-backs to other government agencies. If those agencies don't need training, or don't like the price, OIR loses an opportunity to earn revenue.

The OIR "sold" US$3 million in training to other agencies last year, of which US$1.8 million was funded for information systems employees and US$1.2 million was for end users. The training helps the state by generating competent employees and boosting confidence and morale. It also serves as a perk to retain the many information systems workers tempted by the private sector, according to David Wooten, OIR information systems manager and a former school principal. But the bottom line for OIR is selling the training to other state agencies.

To that end, Wooten's office is now preparing to provide Web-based learning as an alternative to classroom learning. Although it will save state workers time, travel and lost productivity, the state needed a "critical mass" before giving the OIR the green light. A critical mass of students ensures there's enough avoided classroom costs to offset infrastructure and courseware development costs. Wooten and his colleagues decided there was also critical mass in terms of end-stations connected to the network, the network's multimedia capability, its stability, and the fact that online courseware had moved beyond the geewhiz stage into the educationally sound stage.

Wooten said, "What I am certain of is that OIR pays salaries and maintenance and network fees, and buys PCs and network interface cards. If I'm not doing my job, we're out of business."

➤ Teletech

TeleTech, a leading provider of customer relationship management and call center services to the Fortune 500, is rolling out a Web-based learning program to 12,500 customer service agents over the next three years. The company will use the Web to deliver as many as 20 to 25 hours of modular "knowledge bites" on customer service, call handling, leadership and software skills.

Throughout the day, TeleTech's customer relationship management (CRM) platform, CyberCareTM, will automatically fill downtime by launching an interactive online learning lesson on selected agents' screens. When call volume picks up, agents will go back to managing customers. This is a far more efficient use of agents' time than letting them languish during slow periods and pulling them away for classroom training during busy periods.

> *The company will use the Web to deliver as many as 20 to 25 hours of modular "knowledge bites" on customer service, call handling, leadership and software skills.*

TeleTech will also use its e-learning technology, the Pathlore Learning Management System, to turbo-charge recruiting. Prospective employees who submit an electronic resume to the company will simultaneously take an online test to gauge their aptitude for the work. The learning management system will tally the results and embed them in the résumé. When TeleTech needs to hire a new crew of agents, it can cull the best candidates based in part on their scores, avoiding the time and expense of written exams.

Once hired, TeleTech will use the learning management system to assign employees to different curriculums based on their current and potential abilities. A technically savvy agent could skip basic e-mail and Web browsing. An intelligent, outgoing agent might be on the fast-track-to-leadership curriculum. The system delivers all courses automatically.

"We'll also be able to standardize training on our clients' products, services and corporate philosophies while measuring the instructional effectiveness of each lesson — in fact, each question," said Paul Grossi, director of multimedia for Cygnus Computer Associates, TeleTech's Professional Services software development division.

For competitive reasons, the company can't release all of its ROI calculations. But according to Grossi, TeleTech expects to reduce costly instructor-led learning by minimum 25 percent and to "significantly" curb turnover, the bane of the customer care industry. The program will pay for itself in a year — maybe even nine months. "Lots of executives balk at training people just to have them leave the company," Grossi said. "The bottom line, though, is what kind of information will you have if you don't train them and they do end up staying?"

> *...TeleTech expects to reduce costly instructor-led learning by minimum 25 percent and to "significantly" curb turnover, the bane of the customer care industry.*

Statistics back up the wisdom of training customer service agents. Call centers with any kind of learning regimen lasting longer than a month are more than twice as successful at retaining staff compared with call centers having shorter training or none at all, according to the Olsten Corp. (*CallCenter* magazine, January 26, 2000). "Even so, ROI is very difficult to calculate in this industry," Grossi said. "A number of things can cause turnover. To ensure success, the company must be fully committed. We have made a commitment (globally) to provide effective, standardized training to ensure consistency with every customer interaction, and to attract and retain the best employees to manage those interactions.

■ Seven ways to bag ROI

Here are seven things a company can do to lay the groundwork for calculating and securing positive, accurate and persuasive ROI.

1. Consider the solution: Before you even commit to training, identify your business problem and make sure training is the solution. If the problem is inefficiency, maybe faster computers and a more powerful network is the solution,

Figure 1.

Duration of learning	33 hours
Estimated student numbers	750
Period over which benefits are calculated	12 months
COSTS	
Design and development	$40,930
Promotion	$4,744
Administration	$12,713
Faculty	$86,250
Materials	$15,000
Facilities	$40,500
Students	$553,156
Evaluation	$872
Total cost	US$754,165
BENEFITS	
Labor savings	$241,071
Productivity increases	$675,000
Other cost savings	$161,250
Total benefits	US$1,077,321
Return on investment	143%
Payback period	8 months

not a week-long course on mastering Microsoft Office. If all you have is a hammer, then everything looks like a nail. If you're a professional trainer, the world looks like a training problem. It's not always the case.

2. Get a baseline: To calculate training benefits, quantify the "before" picture. Measure everything that training might improve. If you're training 10,000 employees to the basics of sexual harassment in the workplace, take a look at how many employees you have, how many lawsuits were filed over the past five years, insurance premiums and the cost of the penalties.

3. Automate: E-learning management software systems can provide all the necessary data on students, their activities and performance — before and after training whether it occurs online or off.

4. Minimize costs: Since ROI is the ratio of training benefits to costs, you can improve results by lowering the denominator. You can put learning online, limit the number of students, shorten classes, schedule training after work, increase the student/instructor ratio, and minimize custom course development.

5. Maximize training benefits: A similar principle holds true here. Expand the numerator for better ROI. Reinforce training benefits through practice and positive reinforcement like rewards, notes, special honors or even a company wide e-mail. These measures can galvanize results and magnify training effectiveness.

6. Convert soft concepts to hard numbers: This is key. If you're training for productivity, measure the widget output. Don't make widgets? Measure client satisfaction levels before and after training. Work in securities? Measure the cost of SEC fines before and after training. Teaching computer skills? Measure document output, help-desk call reduction, router deployment, or network uptime.

7. Consider the payback period: As convincing as it can be, ROI is just a percentage. To really make it persuasive, convert it to payback time. If a $100,000 training investment is generating $400,000 a year in profit, it's paying for itself in three months. That's a measure anybody can understand. Costs divided by monthly benefits yields the number of months to payback.

■ *Formula for ROI success*

Once a company has laid the groundwork, it can then apply an ROI formula. Training ROI formulas vary, but here's a sound one from Fastrak Consulting Ltd. in the UK.

First, add up costs over the training period for: design and development, promotion, administration, delivery (faculty or technology), materials, facilities, employee wages, lost productivity and evaluation. Then, tally the benefits, including: labor savings, productivity increases, other cost savings (lower maintenance, turnover, debt costs) income generation, new leads, new products. Divide benefits by costs to get ROI. See Table 1 for an example.

With a solid figure for training ROI in hand, managers control their destiny. They improve their chances at securing funding for new, bolder learning initiatives. They have a solid foundation for optimizing the training they're already conducting. And they have a strong connection to the company's bottom line and a business case for their very existence.

Still, it's not always easy quantifying, tracking, capturing, calculating and reporting all the costs and all the benefits around training. Sometimes it's not even worth the trouble (negative ROI). An ROI analysis can simply be too much for the scope of the project, especially if a company is training just a few people over a limited duration. Sometimes, it's good enough just to capture the anecdotal evidence.

If, for instance, the CEO sends the company an e-mail saying the new product training program made a "tremendous difference" in sales and customer satisfaction, save the e-mail, cite it and pull it out when you need it. If the chief technology officer says the network training seems to have "dramatically" reduced network downtime, make it the cornerstone of the business case for the next learning initiative. Then just go with your gut. But if you can get the numbers, you can be certain the learning program will survive another day.

Source: John Martin, "ROI: Do It & Prove It," ASTD Training & Development Magazine (web article), September 2000. Reprinted with permission from the author.

Chapter 21
Measuring Learning and Results

By Thomas J. Falkowski

The types of measures that use to work to evaluate training just don't tell the whole story. Traditional measures like number of employees trained, hours of training per employee, etc., don't accurately address the impact. While they are easy to compile and track, they tend to focus on training rather the real goals of learning and on-the-job performance. In fact, optimizing these measures can actually lead to less than optimal results from your training initiatives.

There is an increasing pressure for training to deliver bottom line results. Unfortunately, most organizations do not take the time to collect real measures on the effectiveness of training and more importantly learning and improvement programs. A comprehensive program includes traditional training, e-learning, electronic performance support, job aids, collaboration tools and coaching and feedback. In order to evaluate the true value of an integrated learning and performance initiative, you need to look across a number of different types of measures. These measures include:

➤ Learner-focused measures

➤ Performance-focused measures

➤ Culture-focused measures

➤ Cost and Return measures

Each of these tells a different part of the whole story.

■ Learner-Focused Measures

These are more traditional type measures. They capture specific feedback from individual learning events. Typically they focus on two areas: learner satisfaction with the learning event and whether or not they have learned the material covered in the learning event. These are good measures to check the effectiveness of course design and delivery; however, by themselves they don't help to indicate whether or not the learning has direct relevance and impact on performance.

Below is a sample measurement plan for learner-focused measures.

LEARNER-FOCUSED MEASUREMENTS			
MEASURE	**UNIT OF MEASURE AND BASELINE**	**GOALS**	**TRACKING MECHANISM**
User Feedback Participant feedback — how well did you like the learning event?	**Measure** Rating of 1 to 9 for session feedback	Average rating of 7	Evaluation forms
User Testing and Assessment How well learners learn the content being presented.	**Measurement** Specific knowledge checks incorporated into the learning	90% correct	Built-in evaluations

■ Performance-Focused Measures

Performance-based measures begin to focus on the relevancy and results of the learning. These measures help to show how well the learning has been targeted to specific organizational performance issues. Some of these measures can be done easily at the learner level, however, the organizational improvement requires a more comprehensive approach. Many organizations are reluctant to invest the time and energy involved to collect this data.

Below is a sample measurement plan for performance-focused measures.

PERFORMANCE-FOCUSED MEASUREMENTS			
MEASURE	**UNIT OF MEASURE AND BASELINE**	**GOALS**	**TRACKING MECHANISM**
Relevancy Participant feedback — how relevant is the learning to your job performance?	Rating of 1 to 9 for session feedback	Average rating of 7	Built-in evaluations
On-the-Job Performance Feedback from both the learner and their supervisor or peers on how well they've incorporated the specific learning into their job and its impact on performance.	Rating of 1 to 9	Average rating of 7	Follow-on evaluations to learners and supervisors or peers. For behavioral training, this is often accomplished through 360° evaluations
Work Group/ Organization Performance	Specific productivity measures. Examples could include things like revenue/employee or throughout	20% improvement	Impact Study

■ Cultural-Focused Measures

One of the powerful aspects of e-learning and the effective use of learning technologies is that through the use of tools like electronic performance support systems, knowledge tools and collaboration tools, the reliance on structured learning can be decreased. The technology actually helps to reduce the need for "formal" training. Traditional measures don't typically capture the impact of these integrated learning solutions. The performance-focused measures can be designed to measure part of the impact but there is also a cultural element. Culture-focused measures help to measure the extent to which individual managers support learning and the extent to which the organization is implementing processes and systems that encourage and support ongoing learning.

Below is a sample measurement plan for cultural-focused measures.

CULTURAL-FOCUSED MEASUREMENTS			
MEASURE	**UNIT OF MEASURE AND BASELINE**	**GOALS**	**TRACKING MECHANISM**
Managers Measures How effectively managers support ongoing learning and development	% favorable ratings	80% favorable	Organizational surveys
Organizational Measures How effectively the organization's systems support ongoing learning, development and performance	% favorable ratings	80% favorable	Organizational surveys

■ Cost and Return Measures

The final area is cost. Costs measures can be extremely beneficial in helping to cost justify investments in learning. They can be used to compare various learning options. Additionally, when combined with performance-focused measured they can tell a powerful story about return on investment.

Below is a sample measurement plan for cost and return measures.

COST AND RETURN MEASUREMENTS			
MEASURE	**UNIT OF MEASURE AND BASELINE**	**GOALS**	**TRACKING MECHANISM**
Learners/Course # of learners per selected courses	# of users per course	Varies by course	LMS
Cost/Course Total cost of selected courses	Total development and delivery cost	Varies	Internal management reports
Cost/Student Per student cost for selected courses	Total development and delivery cost/ total learners	Varies	Internal management reports

■ *Summary*

When combining these four different types of measures, organizations can get an accurate picture of the results of their overall learning strategy. Unfortunately, many organizations don't have the time, resources or desire to put in place a comprehensive measurement plan. That's the bad news. The good news is that there is now wide spread acceptance that traditional measures don't tell the real story: Learning is about performance and results! And, getting results requires an integrated learning strategy tied to your organization's business strategies.

Chapter 22
Online Testing and Evaluation

By Ann D. Yakimovicz

■ Introduction

Testing. Assessment. Evaluation. Those words are popping up with regularity among trainers and human resources managers these days. For trainers, their streamlined companies expect them to show that the expense of training is beneficial to the company; they need to go beyond the traditional "smile sheets" used to measure the satisfaction of training participants. Measuring the learning at the end of training, and again on the job, can help. And these same measures, can work for human resources, too. With labor shortages and continual employee turnover, human resources departments are turning to evaluation as a way to identify knowledge and skill or to assist managers in performance assessments.

Testing, as used in education and sometimes in training, has traditionally been a paper-and-pencil affair, graded by the instructor. It's time-consuming to deliver and to score. And running statistical calculations to determine reliability, validity, and draw broader conclusions from test scores is only done in a limited way, due to the labor demands for inputting all that data.

Now, as companies move more and more of their work to computers, they are reducing time spent on manual data manipulation. First companies shifted to use of Web-based technology to support creation and delivery of products and services, using the Web for data storage and data sharing, then for communication, both internally and externally. Now organizations have begun to utilize the technology, especially via corporate intranets, for improved administrative management — e-learning, payroll systems and employee management systems. As the advantages of these online systems have become clear, training and human resources departments are ready to apply the systems to new uses such as on-line testing and assessment for both self-study and group training programs.

■ What's New About Online Testing?

For some time, simple testing software has been available for standalone computers and on CD-ROMs. So, why are test designers excited about online testing as it can be used in a Web-networked organization? The simple answer is "opportunity." Test designers can see many advantages to automatic storage and presentation of text questions, scoring and storage of results. Computers are well suited to performing complex mathematical calculations. Putting this functionality to work online allows test designers to provide much higher quality tests in eight ways.

Overall randomization is an enormous opportunity. Paper-and-pencil tests present test questions in the same order for every copy of one test version. The pre-determined order creates several problems. A group of test takers in one room must be proctored to insure no cheating occurs when everyone knows the order of the answers is the same. And, questions presented early in a test can sometimes present information used to solve later questions, so the test is not assessing real knowledge adequately.

An online test can handle both of these problems through random presentation of the test questions. Even with a group of learners in the same computer laboratory, the test questions can be presented in very different order to each one, minimizing the possibility of one learner cheating by viewing the answers of another. Also, statistical comparisons can be used to study the order in which certain questions are presented to identify unintentional learning effects.

And, online random-order tests, especially those drawn from a large pool of questions, eliminate one additional problem of paper-and-pencil tests - that of shared copies and advance memorization of test questions. In education, preparation of answers due to early knowledge of the questions happens among students, both individuals and groups. In the workplace, this circumstance can occur in teams, with supervisory or management involvement, particularly if the teams perform similar work and are competitively compared on performance results. When advance knowledge is not possible or useful in the workplace, test results are more meaningful and can more clearly identify areas for performance improvements beneficial to the organization.

An online database provides a second great opportunity. Unlike educational settings, many work settings allow, even require, learners to take a test several times if they do not achieve a passing score at first. Because it is easy to store and retrieve questions from a much larger digital pool than different versions of paper tests, the test question database can insure repeat testers do not see the same questions again. Presenting different questions on the same material helps insure actual knowledge of the material is tested, rather than previous experience with the question.

Third, a large database of questions can be structured for use in another way. Test designers usually start with a table of specifications to proportion the questions among the specific sub-topics in the material trained or studied. In this way, they can assign the appropriate weight for the importance of the sub-topic or the amount of time spent covering it. An online database can maintain several sections, each containing a pool of questions for a sub-topic. When the assessment is administered, a specified number of questions is drawn from each pool and testing is balanced, yielding results that more truly measure actual learning from a training or self-study situation.

... the questions are deliberately designed to clarify a learner's problem-solving approach and identify the point at which errors are more likely to be made.

Adaptive testing, another kind of structure for presenting questions, is a fourth opportunity. In this situation, the computer records answers as the learner makes them, compares the scores to a framework set by the designers, then selects new questions based on the comparison. For example, say the learner selects the correct answer for the first ten questions in a simple math test. The computer compares the learner's score to a range of scores, then presents the learner with more difficult questions. A learner who scored very poorly on the same questions would be presented with additional simpler questions.

Adaptive testing works in two ways. First, it provides a way to challenge and really test the knowledge of better learners. In addition, the questions are deliberately designed to clarify a learner's problem-solving approach and identify the point at which errors are more likely to be made. An instructor, trainer or coach to help the learner correct errors and improve performance can then use this information.

A fifth very exciting difference for online testing is the opportunity to provide immediate feedback to the test taker. Whether responding question-by-question, by groups of questions, or at the end of a complete test, the testing system can tell learners very quickly how well they did, where they made mistakes, and can direct learners to online remediation, enhancing their knowledge and again improving performance for the organization. Because of its hyperlink functionality, web-based testing in particular provides an opportunity to include links to review material, additional exercises or examples, and communication with experts via e-mail, chat or conferencing, then links back to retake test material.

Providing immediate feedback also means the ability to immediately score the test, a sixth opportunity most interesting to training and human resources managers who provide high-level reports to senior management. Test management systems automate the substantial chore of data input for trainers and human resources staff. The systems can also link to online employee management systems for automated record keeping by employee and can deliver detailed statistical analysis of test results. While test developers and statisticians have often used total test scores in determining test quality, item analysis methods to measure the quality of particular test questions has rarely been done. With a test system that automatically performs the calculations and provides these reports, designers can quickly weed out non-discriminating questions. These are the kind, for example, that "everyone" gets right, or wrong. These questions do not adequately discriminate between learners who know the answers and those who do not.

A seventh advantage of online testing is availability. For organizations with staff who work different shifts, online testing is readily available at a time convenient for the employee. Managers no longer have to juggle work team responsibilities to cover for members who are absent to test on another shift; nor is there a problem with employees scoring poorly because they are mentally struggling to keep awake on a testing shift different from their own.

Using Web-based systems to deliver online testing creates one final, unique opportunity. Test questions no longer have to be static text. Questions can include still graphics, animation, audio and video; they can include examples from a company's own records, dynamically generated so they are always up-to-date even as records change. They can link to other parts of an organizational system, if necessary, for both questions and feedback/explanations when scoring.

■ *Limitations of Online Testing*

In education, the biggest question about online testing is, "How do we know the right person is taking the test?" Where instructors are at a distance from the learners, confirming the identity of a test-taker is challenging. Educational institutions have adapted to the use of online testing with password systems, although these can be shared, and with online testing delivered in proctored physical locations. This approach is also used in continuing education programs for professionals, where certification is the result of testing.

In the workplace, the question of "Who's online?" is more easily managed. For one thing, tests are more likely to be administered in the workplace, so a supervisor or test administrator is often present during the test, even if held at an employee's workstation. For another, many organizations have taken steps to control entry into their buildings or into specific work areas, using electronic lock systems and swipe cards that track who entered a location, and when. These swipe cards, with magnetically coded strips similar to credit cards, can also be used with online testing systems. A cubicle, certain computers, even a computer lab, can be set up with a swipe card verification system to confirm a test taker's identity before they are allowed to access the test.

A cubicle, certain computers, even a computer lab, can be set up with a swipe card verification system to confirm a test taker's identity before they are allowed to access the test.

For organizations, the security system for test taking is often verified by human intelligence as well. An employee may be able to gain another employee's swipe card, take the test, and score better than expected in the name of the other employee. However, organizations rarely use one test score for performance management, and a score that's far out of line with expectations serves as a flag to the supervisor to confirm knowledge and performance in other ways.

A second limitation for online testing is employee computer literacy, especially with Web browser functionality and on-screen maneuvering with a mouse. Because online testing systems are built on the Web browser model, they display in ways similar to web pages. Learners must know how to scroll down a "page" if test questions are presented in one lengthy file, how to recognize multiple-choice questions that allow only one answer and those that allow multiple answers, based on the selection mechanism, how to go back and make corrections without losing answers, and how to submit their answers for scoring.

If commercial testing software is used, it must be checked against any and all of the different computer systems and networks in an organization to make sure it will operate correctly in every testing situation as well. Early plans to provide limited online testing in a few locations often get expanded as more and more people discover the value of using the online testing system in numerous ways. Software that starts out as used for testing at the end of new hire orientation suddenly gets used for employee opinion surveys, 360-degree feedback forms, and the newsletter's online scavenger hunt.

■ Ensuring Acceptance and Value

Although online testing seems simple enough, introducing it causes change in organizational processes. As with other change initiatives, anticipate some resistance and identify approaches that can be used to ensure online testing is well accepted.

For an organization seeking to put testing online, first determine how testing is currently used. Consider these questions as a guide to planning:

➤ What kind of testing is done?

➤ Does this testing lend itself to an online format?

➤ Are tests standardized? Are there copyright issues if so?

➤ If not already done, can tests be put in a digital format?

➤ Are tests developed within the company?

➤ What is the internal test development process?

➤ In short, are tests ready to be put online?

➤ If not, can they easily be made ready?

Once organizational readiness is confirmed, focus on users. Today more and more people use a wide variety of wired and wireless devices, with an additional variety of software products, to get their jobs done. Software development companies quickly discovered programmers and computer engineers did not always make the best design decisions for products to be used by consumers and other end-users; they were too expert, too familiar with computers. After some software products failed in the marketplace, development companies led the way in creating the new field of usability studies to learn more about how "real people" would use their software. This approach works well for online testing development, too.

User interface for online tests needs to be an initial consideration. The user interface is what the learner actually sees on the screen. Test takers can be distracted by the color of background or text, by the size of the font in which questions are presented, and by the navigation system they are expected to use to operate the test and orient themselves to answer the questions.

If users are familiar with DOS-based proprietary software, for example, designing an online test that mimics a blue background with white text might be a familiar solution. Creating a user interface to be used internally in the organization also requires the designer to think about color combinations and font size. Overall, approximately 12 percent of the population has some form of color blindness. Attractive screen designs can still be created without limiting color choices, but each should be tested for readability with those who have problems identifying colors, so discrimination is not a problem.

Changes in visual acuity that come with age can also affect test takers. Text and graphic quality in terms of dots-per-inch is much coarser for computer screens than for printed paper. Users can change font size in a browser to control readability, and this function should be allowed to continue in a test document. However, altering font size can affect layout of a test, including placement of questions and answers, resulting in confusion for the learner.

The best way to determine that a user interface will work for the organization or institution is to test it with users. Ask for reactions to different color schemes, check ability to use the navigation functions and to feel in control of the system. If multimedia, such as audio or video, is included in the test, confirm ability to control — back up, stop, replay — these pieces. Commercial testing software companies take some of the guesswork out of user interface design by creating templates into which you add your questions. However, even these templates should be tested with actual users in your organization before using them with tests.

The best way to determine that a user interface will work for the organization or institution is to test it with users.

Once user interface is determined and test questions created, the test can be piloted. Typical pilots start with a content peer group. This group reviews the test for coverage of the content and understanding of the questions. If the group includes managers or supervisors of those to be tested, they can provide valuable critiques of the content and identify information that will be especially valuable to them when they receive test results.

A second pilot is often run with a group of actual users. This group provides a different kind of feedback about the test. First, they will comment on the inherent "fairness" of the test, on whether it checks their real knowledge — not just what supervisors assume they are supposed to know or do, and whether it contains "trick" questions. On completing the test, this group will be either strongly supportive or strongly against the testing, and they will pass the word on to other employees.

Second, this employee pilot group will react to the wording of the test questions. They will describe how and where questions work or are confusing, and their feedback after receiving scores provides information about how well learners will read on-screen. Because of ergonomic discomfort at reading in a vertical position and less-than-perfect screen resolution, readers of all kinds tend to skim online text and skip words. Reaction from this pilot group is an important verification of test question quality and a measure of its likely success. Once the test has been piloted and gained support, it's ready to be implemented, with a continuous cycle for revision and improvement based on regular analysis of the statistical results.

■ What's Next?

Online testing primarily utilizes a multiple-choice, true-false, matching format. As the market for online testing software increases and the programs for data management become more sophisticated, functionality for text-based answers, such as "essay" questions, team-based testing, and synchronous elements, such as live Web-conferencing (audio) and Web-casting (video) will make it possible to use real-life case studies and job-specific situation as part of test procedures. Online testing will become a greater and greater part of providing useful performance evaluations for organizations to make staffing, training, and promotion decisions.

Chapter 23

We Bought into E-learning, Now How Do We Get People to Use It?

By Cliff Carman

The following is a recent posting from an ASTD web discussion group:

> "We have over 1,200 hours of some really great CBTs available to our staff. We did a survey and found only 14 of the 300 people at the site have ever used them. It's pretty bad. What can I do to get these people to want to take these CBTs? How can I get management to encourage them to use them? I really feel we are about to lose this resource if there is no change."

This plea for help echoes the thoughts of many people who have implemented e-learning.

Our Q2 Training objective has been met, our e-learning program is up and running.

■ Congratulations! We're on our way, or are we?

Flash forward to Q4. Employees are only half-completing the courses, or not bothering to log on, or their data is incomplete. The CFO is asking for ROI, and you're wondering whether you're going to be hung out to dry on this project. Motivating online-learning employees to complete or — heaven forbid — start their coursework is the next big challenge for e-learning project managers.

E-learning acceptance in the workplace has caught the attention of the MASIE Center and the American Society for Training & Development (ASTD). Together, they have formed a partnership to understand the critical success factors behind e-learning technologies. Their first joint effort, the "Learning Technology Acceptance Study," will analyze how organizations can increase learner use and acceptance of learning technologies. The study is attempting to determine the conditions under which people are more likely to accept and use technology-based learning. Results of the initial survey are due sometime during the 4th quarter of this year.

Motivating online-learning employees to complete or — heaven forbid — start their coursework is the next big challenge for e-learning project managers.

In the meantime, I would like to share the results of my non-scientific surveys and conversations from corporate training organizations, discussion groups, content providers, and other people who have shared their opinions on the topic.

A recent E*News article discussed how to encourage employees to take advantage of e-learning. There are basically two methods: require e-learning or promote e-learning through marketing techniques. Unless you choose to make the completion of a course mandatory, your marketing effort will be critical to the success of your e-learning program.

◼ *You can lead an employee to water but you can't make 'em drink, or can you?*

Mandated e-learning programs are effective if completion of coursework is considered part of a personal development plan, tied directly to performance reviews, and most importantly related to the performance of a learner's job. My favorite trainer quote about mandated training is…"they (users) hate mandated training that adds no value to their job." Mandating completion of coursework is usually appropriate in cases where your company is required by a regulatory body to file reports showing compliance with a training regulation. The ability to deliver, cost effectively, standard training to an entire organization, makes e-learning a compelling choice. At The Park Avenue Bank, certain training is mandatory and is tied to an employee incentive program. Those who do not complete the required training before their annual review face a financial reduction. Upper Management buy-in for a program that is tied to non-compensation for non-completion is usually simple, but beware of the line manager or supervisor whose lack of support may undermine your efforts. Keep in mind that incorporating a learning management system in your training initiative may help remove the reporting burden from your line managers, and increase their support.

If you are going to mandate e-learning:

➤ Get Upper Management approval,

➤ Don't ask supervisors to administer it,

➤ Make sure the content is relevant to the user's job performance,

➤ Tie course completion to performance reviews,

➤ Make sure everyone has access and the skill to use e-learning, and

➤ Make sure you can track the results.

Most e-learning initiatives have focused on overcoming the challenges of deployment (technology), tracking (Training Management systems), content development (in-house vs. out-sourced), and custom vs. off-the-shelf content. Although not all of the technologies are mature yet, it has not stopped corporations from rolling out e-learning programs. Now that e-learning programs have been implemented, the next generation of challenges has surfaced: getting employees to use it. Most HR organizations do not have the type of management support necessary to mandate the use of e-learning or link its use to job performance objectives.

We know it's in the user's best interest to be proactive about self-development. We did our homework. The content is what the managers said we needed. Then why don't employees use it?

Some problems that keep employees from accepting e-learning are:

➤ They don't even know it exists,

➤ It's not a part of their personal development plans,

➤ It's not part of their performance appraisals,

➤ They don't know how to use it,

➤ They don't know where to get help desk support for e-learning products,

➤ The content is meaningless to them,

➤ The content is boring,

➤ They hate reading online,

➤ They hate being forced to do the training at their desk, too many distractions,

➤ They have no opportunity to give feedback,

➤ They receive no certificate of completion, and

➤ They are all asking themselves the question: What's in it for me?

■ Generate excitement and incentives to promote acceptance

Ask any marketing person and they will tell you it's all in the presentation. Yes, we have done the necessary implementation preparation, now we have to become marketing wizards. Internal promotions are the major key to making everyone aware of the benefits of e-learning.

> Any motivational strategies you use now for other training can be ap-
> plied to Web-based training. By using a computer, some reward struc-
> tures can be automated. In addition, the tracking and reporting avail-
> able with Web-based training allows you to structure rewards and
> requirements for completion and mastery. Students will often need to
> be sold on using something new, and sitting at one's own computer
> doesn't match having free donuts and coffee at a workshop.
> — Brandon Hall

➤ **Management buy-in:**
Be sure to hold demo meetings for managers and supervisors. The objective of the meetings is to show managers the benefits of the program to them as individuals, and in their roles as supervisors. Show the managers how they can

utilize the e-learning offerings as part of their "Management by Objectives," or how e-learning fits into their groups' performance improvement strategy.

➤ **Awareness programs:**

Incorporate e-learning demos in the new hire process. Use instructor-led training events as a place to demo e-learning. Hold cafeteria hands-on sessions with raffles and giveaways for signing up for e-learning events. E-mail is a powerful tool; use it. Place posters in the hallways, function rooms, and every bulletin board. Contests, scavenger hunts (answers only in the e-learning curriculum), and interactive events with your corporate sponsor (the CFO who loves e-learning) are all great tools to promote your e-learning program.

➤ **Follow-up:**

Routinely solicit feedback from users and non-users alike. Effort expended in surveying the audience can uncover hidden complications and result in valuable feedback. Make sure your learning management system gives the users an easy forum for reporting comments about the curriculum and program. When you receive feedback, don't ignore it, even if it's bad news. It's better to change the curriculum at this point than to jeopardize future e-learning initiatives by creating user apathy.

➤ **Content:**

In the content provider world the saying is "content is king." Don't you forget it. No matter how much you promote it, if it looks, smells and tastes like fish sticks, you can't make it caviar. Take the time initially to deduce the objectives of your e-learning program and build or buy content that is aligned with your objectives. Look for interactive content; users do not want to read online. Make sure it's easy to navigate. As learning paradigms shift from training events to continuous learning and performance support, users want to access just the component or learning object they need and get right back to work.

➤ **Recognition:**

What better way than to include completion records in a personnel file? Do your users have the capability to print out certificates of completion? Even if your e-learning management system is linked directly to your HR system (wishful thinking in many cases,) nothing beats the printed certificates to hang proudly in their cubes. Create interdepartmental contests and post the results. The department with the highest completion rate gets the plaque and the good PR. Use your learning portal or Intranet to post congratulatory notes to users on course completion. Use e-mail and send thanks to course users. Create a "wall of fame" to post the pictures of users who have completed an entire certificate program. The list goes on, but you get the idea. Say congratulations loud and clear. Publish your program results, as usage numbers climb, more users will be likely to jump on the bandwagon.

➤ Support:

Make sure users can access a "live person" if they become frustrated trying to use your fancy learning gadget. Once stymied, they may try again. Twice burned, you loose them. Is your e-learning program an icon on the user desktop? Is it easy to get to? Can I call a phone number if I get lost? Ask these and other questions, and make sure you don't just throw the stuff up on the intranet for everyone to use. Just because IT thinks it's intuitive doesn't mean the users do. Recruit help; ask for e-learning mentors or coaches in every department, co-workers who can help users informally on a one-on-one basis. Online chat rooms, mentoring, and support are great tools only if the users knows how to get to them and use them when they are there.

➤ Introducing Change:

If your e-learning initiative is destined to replace traditional classroom training (a move you may regret), be sure to introduce e-learning slowly to supplement your existing traditional training methods. The human need for security manifests itself in resistance to change. Forcing a change will only create greater resistance. Allow traditional learning events to run, and use them to promote e-learning as a supplement.

➤ Earn as you Learn:

Sales people are conditioned to receive incentives for hitting sales goals. Incentives may be in the form of compensation, trips, or recognition. Creating an incentive to direct or modify people's activities can be applied to e-learning. What greater way to promote use of e-learning curriculum than to give your users something for doing it? The "earn as you learn" concept is new to the e-learning space, and there are limited studies to show ROI. However, intuitively we know that users will be more motivated to learn if they earn points toward merchandise in a catalog, or an extra vacation day, or even a mug delivered to their desk. The following press release signifies the first vendor reaction to the "What's in it for me?" question. Conceptually, the idea of earning rewards sounds great, but remember, you have to budget and pay for them.

LEARN2.COM SIGNS EXCLUSIVE STRATEGIC PARTNER-SHIP AGREEMENT WITH MOTIVATION ONLINE COMPANY.
LEARN2.COM INTRODUCES LEARN2.COM PERFORMANCEMO-TIVATOR *as the Missing Link Between E-Learning and Employee Motivation.* Summary: WHiTE PLAINS, N.Y., Mar 22, 2000 /PRNewswire via COM-TEX/ — Learn2.com (Nasdaq: LTWO), a leading provider of e-learning

solutions, and Motivation Online, a leading provider of Internet-based Employee Relationship Management (ERMTM) systems, today signed an exclusive partnership agreement that will combine Learn2.com's e-learning content and Motivation Online's reinforcement and reward performance systems to create a powerful tool for corporate and government organizations. Under the terms of the agreement, Learn2.com will provide Motivation Online with multimedia content for use in its Motivation University, and Motivation Online will provide the engine, links and expertise to Learn2.com for the launch of the Learn2.com PerformanceMotivator. With Learn2.com's Performance-Motivator, you can maximize your employees' use of your web-based training program. PerformanceMotivator provides a direct link between e-learning and motivating employees to participate in online learning initiatives. This is because PerformanceMotivator includes an automatic employee rewards and recognition program that's directly integrated into your Learn2University e-learning package.

With PerformanceMotivator, users are given specific learning objectives and are rewarded with points for meeting and exceeding those objectives. The points are immediately redeemable for products and services from online merchants. Thus, the more course employees complete, the more they learn, the more points they receive, and the more motivated they are to continue improving their skills.

Most training organizations say they like the incentive idea, but no one I know has implemented this type of program to date. However, I think it may become a very powerful change management tool in the future.

■ *How to lead those employees to water*

➤ Management demo meetings

➤ Incorporate e-learning demos in the new hire process

➤ Use instructor-led training events as a place to demo e-learning

➤ Hold cafeteria hands-on sessions with raffles and giveaways for signing up for e-learning events

➤ use e-mail to promote your program

➤ Posters in all public areas and on every bulletin board

➤ Contests, scavenger hunts (answers must be in the e-learning curriculum)

➤ Interactive events with your corporate sponsor

➤ Solicit feedback from users and non-users alike

➤ Don't ignore feedback

➤ Don't forget that "Content is King"

➤ Content must be aligned with the company's e-learning objectives

➤ Content should be interactive

➤ Link completion records to each user's personnel file

➤ Distribute certificates of completion

➤ Create interdepartmental contests and post the results

➤ Post pictures of users who have completed a certificate program

➤ Provide a "live person" for tech support

➤ Introduce e-learning slowly

➤ Offer incentives to e-learning users

In summary, the success of an e-learning program depends more on good old marketing and persuasion than on technological breakthroughs. If you can't mandate e-learning, then be prepared to promote it a lot.

Chapter 24
Trust, Privacy and the Digital University

BY GARY GATIEN

"Organizations today have to be based on trust. How many people can you know well enough to trust? Probably 50 at most."
— Charles Handy, author, management philosopher and consultant to multinational corporations (Rapoport, 1994).

The Digital University

Broadly speaking, the words "digital university" refer to the successful migration of many key activities from paper-based methods to digital methods. A successful migration means not only that universities will be able to improve the means by which they do things now, but also that they and their constituencies will have opportunities to do things that they could not do before.

While this migration includes the assimilation of e-commerce (the buying and selling of products and services electronically) into our institutions, it also includes many other "e-activities." We are migrating to a digital world that comprises, for example:

➤ Online applications and payment of admissions fees,

➤ Campus-wide, integrated administrative computing systems and, eventually, integrated administrative and academic computing systems,

➤ Online purchasing and loan programs,

➤ Online recruiting of students, staff and faculty,

➤ Web access and interaction with personal (including medical) information,

➤ Multi-institutional and consortia-based educational models,

➤ Web-based courses and testing,

➤ Virtual communities,

➤ Online, collaborative research,

➤ Online auctions of university intellectual property,

➤ Digital library resources, and

➤ Electronic grant and development initiatives.

As we migrate, we fundamentally change the way we fulfill our mission. In the future, our constituents will have quick, electronic, and often interactive access to a variety of institutional data and information. Trust will often be based on electronic interactions rather than face-to-face meetings or personal relationships. If we are successful, our institutions will continue to enjoy the trust of our many constituents while remaining competitive in an increasingly global and multi-faceted higher education environment.

■ *The Importance of Trust*

In today's evolving digital universities, the key to success is "trust." Trust is fundamental for many reasons. First, the rapid pace of technology innovation can mean that technological change often takes place before we understand its potential implications. For example, what impact, if any, do the hundreds of commercially-sponsored campus Web sites and "smart cards" (Van Der Werf, 1999) have on our responsibilities under the Family Educational Rights and Privacy Act of 1974 (NCES, 1998; CAUSE, 1997)? How — and how well — are we protecting faculty and institutional intellectual properties, including course notes, syllabi, and research on web sites? From an institutional perspective, how can we best address intellectual property ownership and royalty issues and manage potential conflicts of interest? Consider the following:

➤ *There is no model for migration that we can follow.* In the area of distance education alone, some higher education institutions have entered into a variety of partnerships with for-profit companies, some have joined non-profit educational consortia, some have done both of these and are also delivering courses directly to students, and others have formed for-profit subsidiaries. Faculty are breaking new ground outside of their institutions (Marcus, 1999). Furthermore, the unique circumstances at each of our institutions — including our different missions, strengths and weaknesses, funding levels, cultures, concerns, constituencies, tolerances for risk, infrastructures and approaches to outsourcing — may preclude the development of a single model that will work for all of us.

> *... the unique circumstances at each of our institutions ... may preclude the development of a single model that will work for all of us.*

➤ *There is no coherent set of laws, regulations, and policies on the handling of digital data and information*, nor rules for enforcement, that have withstood (or not been amended by) diverse challenges over time. In fact, these rules are just now being developed at the state, national, and international levels among governments, interest and advocacy groups and trade organizations.

➤ *We are facing issues that we have never had to face before.* For example, customer "profiling" (Dembeck, 1999) and "targeted marketing" (Tedeschi, 1999) were virtually impossible, or at least much less sophisticated, prior to the digital revolution. Today, a person's offline and online buying habits can be merged. Private data can be obtained easily (Penenberg, 1999). A vendor can interrupt students working at their computers through dinner by sending them a pop-up window offering to sell them pizza (Woody, 1999).

➤ *When things go wrong online, it is the credibility of institutions that's at stake*, not just the reputations of registrars, accounts offices, schools or colleges, or individual units. In industry parlance, it's our "brand name" that is at risk.

➤ *Finally, trust is key because a successful migration to a digital university requires that we build new, "electronic relationships."* In some cases, we will want to build communities through viable, long-term relationships with people that we have not met face-to-face. We will need partnerships with all of our constituencies to share risk and reward so that we may all take advantage of the opportunities that technology offers.

The Charles Handy quotation that opened this chapter helps to put into perspective the scope and complexity of the migration that we face. That's because we need to build trust not simply among 50 people, but rather among hundreds, even thousands, of people: a highly diverse, global audience that includes faculty, students, and staff as well as parents, alumni, donors, sponsors, vendors, partners, collaborators, governments and educational institutions.

Two recent surveys of e-commerce — an area in which traditional institutions of higher education lag way behind businesses, government, commercial education providers and society in general — highlight the importance of trust. Jupiter Communications found that 64 percent of survey respondents do not trust a web site to offer privacy even if there is a privacy policy posted on the site. Jupiter also projected that privacy issues could put an US$18 billion dent in the US$40 billion e-commerce revenue the communications firm predicts will accumulate by 2002. According to Michael Slack, a Jupiter analyst, "It's not just about having legislation or privacy policy postings. There is a general nervousness about giving personal and credit card information on the Net" ("Industry Privacy Failures," 1999).

Similarly, NFO Interactive found consumer concern about the safekeeping of online personal information to be the main reason people chose not to shop online. Consumers said that what would most entice them to shop at a Web site was "trust that the site would keep personal information private" ("Industry Privacy Failures," 1999). Another survey suggests that to address trust successfully, we need to explore this issue with our constituents in more detail than we have done so far (Cranor, et al, 1993). Business-to-business (B2B) e-commerce is also struggling to ensure trust and minimize litigation (Hicks, 1999). It's no wonder that privacy is reportedly becoming the new "e-industry;" some experts anticipate that security lawsuits will replace Y2K litigation over the next few years (Mosquera, 1999).

■ Selected Actions To Help Ensure a Successful Migration

While each of our institutions will have to develop and refine these actions according to individual circumstances, below are some suggestions for the mission, guidelines, and action steps of a migrating institution.

➤ **Mission:** To build an integrated, proactive, extended enterprise of education, knowledge discovery, co-invention, and community outreach.

➤ **Guidelines:** First, ensure that needs, desires, policies, and concerns drive technology selections, not the other way around. Second, within institutions, work cooperatively across functional areas (e.g., administrative, academic, research, etc.). Third, work collaboratively with peer institutions. Fourth and finally, provide Web-based constituency access via an interface that is easy to use, easy for users to customize, consistent in its functions, robust in terms of the data and information it provides, secure, and ADA compliant.

➤ **Selected Actions:** The National Center for Education Statistics recommends that higher-education executives raise the visibility of electronic privacy and security issues and appoint a campus leader for institution-wide privacy and security policy (NCES, 1998). Others recommend improved privacy and security education across campuses. For example, a 1998 FBI/Computer Security Institute survey found that the average loss for security breaches ranged from US$2.8 million for "unauthorized insider access" to just US$86,000 for "system penetration by an outsider" (Zimits & Montano, 1998).

Not all data and information require the same levels and kinds of protection. Moreover, resources are not infinite. Consensus-building among constituencies is one way to help determine priorities.

■ Conclusion

Higher education institutions are becoming digital universities. To migrate successfully, we need to address proactively the role and importance of an "old-fashioned" value, namely trust, in the digital world. We must proceed with a clear mission and guidelines and take concrete actions based on collaborations with our constituencies. We will likely face some common technical, policy, privacy, security, and legal issues. However, we will likely find as well that a successful migration requires unique approaches and solutions.

Source: Gary Gatien, "Trust, Privacy, and the Digital University," Technology Source, May/June 2000. Reprinted with permission of the author.

■ References

Cause Task Force, "Privacy and the Handling of Student Information in the Electronic Networked Environments of Colleges and Universities," 1997. Retrieved June 1999 from the World Wide Web: http://www.educause.edu/asp/doclib/abstract.asp?ID=pub3102

Cranor, L., J. Reagle & M. Ackerman, "Beyond Concern: Understanding Net Users' Attitudes About Online Privacy," 1993, April. Retrieved December 1999 from the World Wide Web: http://www.research.att.com/projects/privacystudy/

Dembeck, C., "Is It Customer Profiling or Harassment?" *E-Commerce Times*, 1997, July 7. Retrieved from the World Wide Web: http://www.ecommercetimes.com/news/viewpoint/view-990707.shtml

Hicks, M. "A Matter of Trust," *PC Week* Online, 1999, October 25. Retrieved November, 1999 from the World Wide Web: http://www.zdnet.com/pcweek/stories/news/0,4153,2376988,00.html

"Industry Privacy Failures Hurting E-Commerce, Latest Surveys Show," 1999, September 9, *Privacy Times*. Retrieved 10 September 1999 from the World Wide Web: http://www.privacytimes.com/NewWebstories/indus_priv_9_9.htm

Marcus, A., "Why Harvard Law Wants to Rein in One of Its Star Professors." *The Wall Street Journal*, 1999, November 22, pp. A1, A10.

Mosquera, M. "Security Lawsuits to Replace Y2K Litigation," *TechWeb*, 1999, November 17. Retrieved November 1999 from the World Wide Web: http://www.techweb.com/wire/story/TWB19991117S0005

National Center For Education Statistics (NCES), "Task Force Safeguarding Your Technology," 1998, September 22. Retrieved June 1999 from the World Wide Web: http://nces.ed.gov/pubs98/safetech/

Penenberg, A. L., "The End of Privacy." Forbes, 1999, November 29. Retrieved December 1999 from the World Wide Web: http://www.forbes.com/Forbes/99/1129/6413182a.htm

Rapoport, C., "Charles Handy Sees the Future," *Fortune*, 1994, October 31, pp. 155-168.

Tedeschi, R., "Targeted Marketing Confronts Privacy Concerns," *The New York Times* on the Web, 1999, May 10. Retrieved 23 June 1999 from the World Wide Web: http://www.nytimes.com/library/tech/99/05/cyber/commerce/10commerce.html

Van Der Werf, M., "A Vice President from the Business World Brings a New Bottom line to Penn." *Chronicle of Higher Education*, 1999, September 3, pp. A72-75.

Woody, T., "Back to School in the Internet Economy," *The Industry Standard*, 1999, August 6). Retrieved 6 August 1999 from the World Wide Web: http://www.thestandard.net/articles/display/0,1449,5812,00.html

Zimits, E. & C. Montano, "Public Key Infrastructure: Unlocking the Internet's Economic Potential," *iStory* 3 (2), 1998, April. Retrieved June 1999 from the World Wide Web: http://www.iword.com/iword32/istory32.html

E-learning Future

Chapter 25
Learning at the Speed of Light

By Jeff Creighton

There is no question that Web-based learning is having a profound impact on how we, as a society, acquire and master new skills and absorb information. E-learning technologies provide access to learning opportunities 24 hours a day, seven days a week. We now have the beginnings of a technology revolution that will help futurists and management gurus like Peter Drucker realize their vision of the "knowledge society," where what we know, both individually and organizationally, becomes the new basis for economic value. "The continuing professional education of adults is the No. 1 gross industry in the next 30 years, but not in the traditional form," states Drucker. "In five years, we will deliver most of our executive management programs online." According to Doug Donzelli, the CEO of Pensare, "The core of e-knowledge, the Internet, will "democratize" learning, providing greater access at lower cost, ultimately improving quality."

So, at this point, I'd like to make a somewhat bold statement about my view on the future of distance learning; I believe we are years away from providing an experience that will deliver the same outcomes as those of the traditional classroom, and we may never get there. And we don't have to. Both types of learning delivery will have a solid place in the education map of the future.

■ Learning vs. Education

I believe that we have ill-defined expectations for e-learning, and have used these expectations as a comparison to traditional learning models. We are asking both to achieve similar outcomes when both models should be used by individuals and organizations to achieve different outcomes.

I am going to attempt to differentiate e-learning in fact all learning, from traditional education.

E-learning can stand on its own as a powerful model to help individuals acquire new skills, and advance the skills they already have. E-learning will transform training in a way that we've never seen previously. In fact, it already has. "The e-knowledge market will enjoy explosive growth, reaching US$53.3 billion by 2003 from US$9.4 billion in 1999," according to Merrill Lynch.

I no longer just take in information, I analyze it, process it, and form opinions that will impact my decisions based on the education I have received.

But the skills acquisition that lends itself to the e-learning model leads to outcomes that are different from traditional higher education, and companies have very different expectations on their training outcomes than do universities on their degree-based educational programs.

Education, as I define it, goes beyond the acquisition of knowledge and skills found in e-learning. Education leads to a transformation in the individual's analytical skills and their world view. Education literally changes the person's filter for processing information. I no longer just take in information, I analyze it, process it, and form opinions that will impact my decisions based on the education I have received. This type of education forms the foundation for all future learning.

Today e-learning has not proven itself capable of leading to these outcomes, and I question whether it should attempt to accomplish these outcomes. This is the role that traditional education takes in our society, when we have the time and immersion required to truly change the way we view the world and our analysis of it. Most of us have completed this process by the time we're in our early twenties. We've immersed ourselves in college, and whether we know it or not, we've come out a different person.

While e-learning does not result in this type of transformation, it is incredibly valuable in delivering high-impact skills acquisition primarily due to its "just-in-time" delivery. According to Merrill Lynch, the just-in-time nature of e-learning can lead to skills retention of up to 250 percent greater than that with classroom-based learning.

■ *The Education Map*

The education map displayed here identifies various modes of learning delivery and expected outcomes. Of course, within most models there are exceptions to the rule, but for the vast majority of cases, the mapping of learning delivery method to expected outcomes holds true.

All learning begins with an individual's fundamental beliefs about the world in which he/she lives and operates. These fundamental beliefs form the basis from which all future experiences will be processed, analyzed, and stored. All future learning will be filtered through this core set of beliefs obtained through experiences and education. Up to this point, traditional classroom-based education has formed the foundation for an individual's belief set that they will use to process all future learning. There are a number of reasons why this setting leads to these outcomes, and we could spend years studying the theories that support these claims, but let me highlight two that I deem critically important: immersion and interaction.

Most of the educational "Ah Ha's", as I call them, that occur in our lives and form the foundation of our core beliefs happen when others challenge our beliefs. These interactions can occur between faculty and student, or student-to-student, but they occur when our belief set is challenged. The fundamental point is that people change our core beliefs, not technology. And this process takes time. Why do most universities require that CEOs stay on campus for two weeks of intense leadership development? It's because these highly-respected executive education providers want to challenge CEOs' beliefs about the world,

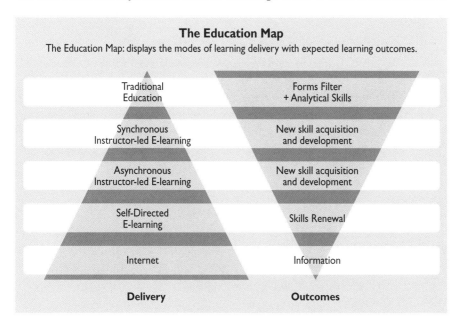

The Education Map

The Education Map: displays the modes of learning delivery with expected learning outcomes.

Delivery	Outcomes
Traditional Education	Forms Filter + Analytical Skills
Synchronous Instructor-led E-learning	New skill acquisition and development
Asynchronous Instructor-led E-learning	New skill acquisition and development
Self-Directed E-learning	Skills Renewal
Internet	Information

business and leadership. They want to challenge core beliefs, knowing that all learning by that CEO will be improved in the future. Education providers understand that they can't accomplish this through technology, but only through immersion and interaction. Christos Cotsakos, CEO of E-trade, has this to say regarding his traditional MBA experience, "My MBA taught me how to change the rules of engagement, and then, ultimately, change the game."

The closest online comparison to our traditional education model is what is known as synchronous learning, where an instructor is teaching online in real-time, and is available during that time to answer questions. Synchronous learning involves communication with students and faculty with no time delay. Synchronous interaction can occur via the telephone, chat, and Internet telephony. Synchronous learning is moving in the direction of achieving similar outcomes to traditional classroom-based education, but has yet to achieve these outcomes due to lack of the immersion and quality of interaction needed to truly challenge a person's core belief systems.

The Internet will drive our learner-centric society into the future. But information and education, although not mutually exclusive, do not share all of the same properties.

The remaining parts of the education map are comprised of asynchronous learning and self-paced learning. Asynchronous learning involves student-to-student and student-to-teacher communication that is "time-delayed" — separated by minutes, hours, even days. Correspondence courses and e-mail are asynchronous forms of e-learning. These are particularly adept at helping the student hone current skills, or learn new ones. Corporations are quite successful in employing these models extensively to provide employees with "just-in-time" learning opportunities that are directly applicable to the job at hand.

At the base of the education map is the Internet itself — the new information medium for the coming age. At the core of the Internet is information. And information makes up a key source of learning capital. The Internet is to our society what the printing press was to the middle ages: a complete information revolution. The Internet will drive our learner-centric society into the future. But information and education, although not mutually exclusive, do not share all of the same properties.

I believe that the most interesting developments in education delivery are the hybrid offerings, combining the power of e-learning with the immersion and interaction of the traditional classroom. Many of these programs have been developed in our prestigious universities. They have intense residency requirements where students are working together on campus over a period of weeks.

The students then return to their jobs and lives. They continue in their studies and interaction utilizing the power of the Internet for communication, research and submission of assignments. These programs are fairly new, and we have yet to see their results in developing the analytical skills of more traditional delivery methods, but all indications are that these programs will be successful.

■ *The Measurement of Learning vs. Education*

If we accept that education and learning are different in the ways I have defined them previously, we can better develop models to measure the effectiveness of each.

Learning and e-learning can be measured by their ability to meet certain objectives, either set by the organization sponsoring the learning, the individual, or learning providers themselves. Many income/outcome assessment models have been defined to measure the effectiveness of these types of programs. The fundamental approach is to base the value of learning on its ability to teach the skills defined in the course objectives. Skills-based learning is easily measured through post-course testing that determines whether the student mastered the skills identified in the course.

The challenge occurs when we attempt to apply these same income/outcome assessment models to education programs such as undergraduate and graduate degree programs. These education programs deliver outcomes leading to problem solving and analytical skills. If we attempt to use this singular income/outcome assessment model, what we end up receiving on behalf of employees is not a paradigm shift to a new way of processing information, but a new or enhanced set of skills. And for many organizations paying the bill for their employees' degrees, this is an ample model for measuring the effectiveness of these programs. Unfortunately, if we apply this model as the definitive benchmark for educational offerings, we end up with degrees at a distance that are nothing more than skills-based training programs, delivering on the course objectives but fostering no paradigm shift for the employee enrolled in the program.

Patrick O'Boyle, a 39-year-old account manager for Parabon Computation who finished the coursework for his bachelor's degree at an online program had this to say about the success of his experiences: "I can say without reservation that every course I took turned into dollars for me in business."

So what should we measure? We should measure that which we can measure.

The primary argument for measuring our educational investment is the concept that education as finite. All degrees represent a series of courses intended to transfer a common body of knowledge. All accredited MBA programs, for example, have a common body of knowledge, being finance, marketing, accounting, and economics. Mastery of these topical areas is measurable. Companies will develop Education Return On Investment (EROI) tools around what is measurable on a quantitative level, and on a qualitative level.

The goals of the corporation and the university delivering an MBA are the same; to develop better managers with the skills to lead people through change. The most effective way for corporations to measure the return on education is to employ an input/output assessment that covers the quantitative and qualitative aspects of an effective manager. Here are the basic tenets of the EROI model as it should formulate itself within corporations:

1. Quantitative Measurements

The quantitative aspects of an MBA program (e.g. accounting, marketing, finance, economics, etc.) can be measured before a participant begins an MBA program using a test that encompasses these skills. The employee is tested before and after the MBA experience, and the change, or delta, represents the effectiveness of the institution in delivering these skills.

2. Qualitative Skills

The qualitative aspects of the program are more difficult to measure, but not impossible. These include management soft skills, leadership qualities, and an ability to analyze problems. Many companies could begin to measure these attributes using current 360 feedback processes. This can be accomplished through an assessment of the person's management skills by his peers, subordinates and bosses. This assessment should be done on the front end of the business program, and again months after the individual has completed the program. The difference between these two assessments gives a benchmark for the effectiveness of the program in delivering on these qualities.

In conclusion, stakeholders in the future of e-learning should continue to measure those aspects of programs that can be measured, including assessing the outcomes achieved. Today, these are primarily skills outcomes, which are well-suited for the e-learning modes of delivery.

E-learning is not yet delivering on the immersion or interaction required to change a student's paradigm for future learning, developing analytical and problem solving skills. These attributes are best developed through more traditional classroom-based education, although a number of hybrid e-learning/classroom programs have evolved to try and bridge the gap.

Chapter 26
Higher Education in 2010:
An Interview
with Rodney L. Everhart

BY JAMES L. MORRISON

Rodney L. Everhart has served as President of SCT Education Solutions, a provider of soft-ware and services to higher education worldwide, since January 1, 1998. Everhart previously was CEO and President of LEXIS-NEXIS Information Services, as well as Senior Vice President of Bellcore, the world's largest telecommunication software and services company.

James Morrison (JM): *Rod, paint us a picture of higher education in the year 2010. What will be the mix of virtual and residential institutions, and how will schools use information technology tools in teaching and administration? Where will we be with distance education?*

Rod Everhart (RE): In the relatively near future, there will be a greater mix of virtual and residential learning. Many courses will be offered both in the traditional classroom and in a virtual environment. Students will choose which of these two environments they want to learn in and which learning style is better for them for each particular course. Students living on campus (in residence halls) will attend some classes in person, but they also will be able to take some courses via the PCs in their rooms. For a particular course, one student might think, "I have a good foundation and background in this subject. I understand what this is, and I can breeze through this in three weeks on my own time." For the same subject, other students might say, "I need personal reinforcement and day-to-day interaction with the professor and other students around me. I want to be in the classroom because I can absorb more in that environment." Furthermore, almost every classroom will have multimedia delivery access available, so students and professors will tap into the Internet for information. Remote access in the classroom will support contact with and learning from various lecturers and experts.

Distance education is a misnomer; "connected learning" is a better term for the virtual interactions we are describing. To me, "connected learning" describes the educational environment that takes advantage of technology to deliver content meaningful to the learner. "Virtual learning" has taken on the context of almost purely Internet-delivered content, and generally this implies large distances between the source and the learner.

Connected learning takes on a broader connotation and role. For example, a professor in a classroom might tap into a digital set of microbiology slides from the world renown expert in this field, or a nuclear physics professor might go into a nuclear power plant for a classroom interactive interview with the facility technology officer while he demonstrates how critical operations are handled. This is taking advantage of "connected learning." Another example might be a student on campus who does his or her homework online within an interactive database that follows avenues where the student is weakest and needs the greatest help, and skips through areas where strength is already evident. Finally, the truly distant learner who takes a course entirely through Internet delivery is a "connected learner," and a "virtual learner," too.

... the truly distant learner who takes a course entirely through Internet delivery is a "connected learner," and a "virtual learner," too.

Considerable evidence indicates that the growing number of adult learners will double the number of learning hours needed by the total student population. Delivering instruction in a traditional sense to that entire population would require doubling the number of campuses, classrooms and professors. That is impossible: no economic plan could fund it, and there are not enough available professors or educational support staff for that kind of a solution. Therefore, if it is true (and I believe that it is) that ours is becoming a knowledge-worker economy — and that there are 141 million knowledge workers who must refresh their skills with formal education on a continual basis — then approximately half of all instruction just has to be delivered as virtual, or "connected," learning. I do not foresee universities doubling the number of campuses and professors. Instruction has to be leveraged, and virtual delivery is a great way to achieve that leverage.

JM: *Certainly more people want to be able to access instruction for lifelong learning. But one thing that all education organizations face is the fact that technology costs money. Wiring costs money, equipment costs money and software costs money.*

RE: But that investment is being made. More and more universities are installing fiber-optic backbones throughout their campuses, and they're doing that for a couple of reasons. They want to support their employees and staff better. PCs are on every worker's desk now, and these computers have graphical user interfaces that require higher bandwidth and decent server support. Although not all universities currently have the infrastructure in place to support staff PCs, most at least plan to upgrade their technological capabilities. So the infrastructure is being planned, and in many cases, put in and paid for. The concern then becomes delivery to individuals. Not every home has the capabilities that I am talking about; therefore, in many cases, universities must provide computer labs and computer access. It is getting to the point that most people who want access to the Internet can find a way to get it. Once they have access to the Internet, then advances like connected learning are possible.

JM: *What new technologies do you see on the horizon that colleges and universities can use to increase their effectiveness and efficiency?*

RE: I am excited about the capabilities of Campus Pipeline, a company located in Salt Lake City. It has a partnership with SCT and connection to the SCT databases. The company's product, also called Campus Pipeline, is an enterprise information portal (EIP) that effectively creates a home base, or a home communication center, for each student or alumnus. It has access to a host of information that fits each constituent's preferences. Say, for example, that a student wants various news, sports, or weather items. Campus Pipeline can deliver those items from the Internet to that student, to his/her specification. It also can provide the student with access to the Internet for searching and researching all kinds of information. Through Campus Pipeline, students can access course catalogs, their grades, their transcripts, and any information in the school database that relates to them personally. Moreover, the company can feed information that schools would like their students to know — for example, the schedule for registering for classes — to individual constituents.

An EIP like Campus Pipeline is one level up from a portal such as Excite or Yahoo or America Online because it seamlessly integrates the power and access of the Internet with the security and personalization of campus information systems. This combination provides 24-hour access to campus and Internet resources and goes beyond the traditional Internet portal with role-based personalization, security, and ease of use. For example, it can provide a course catalog to students based on what they need. If a college senior, for example, goes online to register for classes, the university's registration system can know what the student's degree program is, what courses he/she has taken and needs to take in order to graduate, and what courses he/she would likely choose from. Therefore, the course catalog that students can get on a preferential basis is very specific to them. Can students go off and look at the rest of the course catalog and ask for Basket Weaving 101? Yes, they can. But the catalog is tailored to them individually. These kinds of capabilities greatly strengthen the relationship the institution has with students. Campus Pipeline also strengthens the relationship that institutions have with alumni. EIP services are available to alumni for the rest of their lives, so an alumnus can access Campus Pipeline to take a virtual course that updates his/her skills. Because of this link, when a university sponsors fundraising campaigns, the ties fostered through such a communication and service tool increase the likelihood that alumni will donate funds to the school.

JM: *Many teachers may be troubled by the picture of the "solitary learner" being directed through a course based on pre-programmed response patterns in that this seems to remove the elements of serendipity and accidental discovery that have long been prized in academia. What can you say to these people?*

RE: Connected learning courses can be structured in many, many ways. With that flexibility comes the opportunity for truly innovative, challenging and rewarding programs, and also the reverse. Minds can be expanded and motivated to go down unique paths, or they can be forced through narrow, pre-programmed channels. However, isn't this true in the classroom today? From my perspective, this is where the outstanding professors shine, and likewise, they will shine in a connected learning world. A potential advantage of the virtual world is that the more introverted personalities tend to communicate better in written form than verbal, and they tend to compete on a more equal intellectual footing. They become more involved in digitized discussion threads or chatrooms than they do when faced with potentially intimidating and more exuberant peers in the classroom. The trick, of course, is for the professor to design the course to have that interactive element. Some connected learning courses, for example, use hardcopy textbooks and course materials, just as if in a physical classroom, but the virtual classroom world is entirely comprised of a chat room and a discussion-thread environment. Every course is unique and invigorating to the professor because the discussion threads are never alike. And at the end of every course, the virtual content is "thrown away" and the next class starts with a clean screen.

JM: *A decade ago, the U.S. Army Research Institute considered instituting a system in which an officer assigned to a new duty could, completely via satellite, communicate with his/her branch school, get an assessment test for any knowledge gaps related to the new duty, access material that he/she needed to learn, and get competency tested on that material. Do you know of anything in higher education that is providing continuing professional development like this?*

RE: Yes, it's happening with the lifelong learning capabilities that can be delivered via the Internet.

By the way, there is a big difference between course materials that are tailored for electronic delivery and materials that are made for classroom delivery. When a course is delivered in electronic form, there are a variety of assessment formulas that can be applied as a student responds to questions or takes quizzes that are embedded in the data. If a program has the electronic capability to let you pick and choose answers to questions, and to give you responses that drive you down alternative decision trees, then that program can start to distinguish what it is you know and don't know. For example, let's suppose that there is a reasonably high-level question. If the student answers it correctly, the machine can presume that the student knows a whole series of other things because he/she is able to answer this top-level question correctly. And if the student answers it incorrectly, then the machine knows that it needs to backtrack in order to determine the student's knowledge level.

With these types of programs, learning becomes very personalized, and students can be taken through a course expeditiously. In other words, students can spend time on what they don't know and what they need to know, rather than on what they already know. Many students who have a fundamental knowledge of the basics can skip the basics, and the course content will provide only the instruction needed. Yet behind the scenes, all of the course content is there for any direction in which anybody needs to go.

Let me tell you a personal story. I painfully sat through a semester course called Money and Banking that I probably could have gone through in two weeks on my own. I had to go to class for attendance reasons even though it was not a good learning experience for me. What I did learn, I learned on my own. If I could have taken this course on the Internet, it would have saved me a lot of time that I could have used more productively.

The problem with using videoconferencing in a "live classroom" environment is that students and teachers must appear in a room at a certain time for information delivery.

JM: *Rod, let's return to developments in technology to conclude this interview. Internet 2 is becoming more widely available, and, with its greater bandwidth, will facilitate video conferencing and enhance the ability of educators to transport a classroom from one site to another far more effectively and less expensively than in the past. How do you regard the potential of this technology for enhancing learning?*

RE: The problem with using videoconferencing in a "live classroom" environment is that students and teachers must appear in a room at a certain time for information delivery. This lack of flexibility is unattractive. Videoconferencing doesn't take advantage of the capabilities of new information technologies to provide unlimited access to information available when and how students want it. Under some circumstances, asynchronous technologies may well be more effective in a learning environment than synchronous technologies, particularly from a practical perspective.

Many people expect that the learning world will divide into two camps: Classroom and Virtual. As I've indicated earlier, I think the more likely outcome is a blend. And certainly over a lifetime, the learner will definitely have some of each, often at essentially the same time. I feel the same about synchronous versus asynchronous delivery of content in an electronic sense. The obvious advantages of asynchronous delivery is the "anytime, anywhere" aspects that fits the learners' schedules and allows a good option for conflicts. That flexibility of taking a course at 2 a.m., or after work (whenever that ends) on Thursday night, or on Saturday afternoons when the favorite team isn't on TV, is a major plus. The limitation, of course, is the real-time interaction with others, whether the professor, teammates on a group project, or classmates in general. Some successful professors are finding great value in mixing asynchronous with synchronous. For example, the course starts and ends at the same time for everybody. For the most part, the students do their homework and study on their own schedules and to their own habits. They can jump into the fray of a discussion thread any time day or night, for example. But the professor also schedules a few fixed schedule events: a review session prior to an exam, the exam itself, or even a closing dinner that brings all the participants together face-to-face. The professor also works in a project involving groups of three or four students where sufficient brainstorming is required that the groups meet via phone or in person to accomplish the assignment.

JM: *Asynchronous learners become independent learners. Independent learning — having people think for themselves and figure things out for themselves — certainly is an educational objective.*
RE: I love that thought. Historically, educators have realized the importance of perpetual learning, but the mass population hasn't. In this new environment, everyone has to be a perpetual (or lifelong) learner, and everyone has to want to learn rather than be forced to learn. Nobody can force education.

JM: *Thank you, Rod, for sharing your vision of higher education in 2010.*

Source: James Morrison, "Higher Education in 2010: An Interview with Rodney L. Everhart," Technology Source, November/December 1999. Reprinted with permission of the author.

Chapter 27
Via Technology to Social Change!

By Alan Cummings

Over the past few years, education and training programs have been subject to massive change. Technology not only has altered today's information environment, but also has fundamentally redirected the course of the future. One likely and drastic result will be the unification of the worlds of business and education. Consider the following scenario, which shows what changes may result in 15 to 20 years from this union.

■ The Online Learning Revolution

It is now 2020. Two instructors — with distinct job functions and career structures — manage the classroom.

➤ A class supervisor reviews computer-aided learning (CAL) software for currency, ensures that computers are working, delivers non-key or supplementary learning materials, oversees examinations, collates and reviews learning and attainment records, and fosters a learning environment within the classroom.

➤ A highly qualified, highly paid, teacher delivers the key learning that is not available (or that is considered unsatisfactory) online and contextualizes learning materials against specific local culture or social norms. He/she also works with disabled or special needs students.

The teacher oversees the work of the class supervisor; the former validates learning and assessment records, evaluates the effectiveness of particular learning programs, and reviews the documents (e.g., attendance, performance, and funding records) collated by the class supervisor.

Schools are established on small premises near parents' workplaces or in converted houses that are within walking distance of children's homes. For children older than 10, daily attendance in schools is noncompulsory. Some of the older pupils attend school only twice weekly to get tutorial support from the class supervisor and instruction from the teacher. For the most part, pupils are encouraged to work online from home (like many of their parents) by using teleconferencing tools provided by corporate sponsors. Sponsorship became popular when state schools, underfunded and understaffed for years, became unable to keep pace with the scope of technological change and the requirements of industry. The government now encourages industrial sponsors (with tax breaks, etc.) to supplement state educational funding by providing vocationally-related teaching materials. Each child has to apply for sponsorship; there is fierce competition for support from "superior" patrons.

The government now encourages industrial sponsors (with tax breaks, etc.) to supplement state educational funding by providing vocationally-related teaching materials.

Students older than 10 must complete a minimum number of study hours per year; however, they may accrue these hours at home, in whatever way suits the family schedule. Because their study schedules are flexible, students can maintain regular contact and close relationships with friends, neighbors, and family. Moreover, they can log-on early or late in the day and join live classes in other countries. In order to ensure that each student is learning adequately, computerized audit software automatically monitors: (1) how many hours per week each student studies online, and (2) each student's learning materials and assessment activities. Reports are available to teachers and parents. Because sponsors reward academic success with prizes, job offers, and other perks, free access to online materials is capped. After a student reaches his or her weekly limit, a fee per module is charged — by the state for basic education materials, or by the sponsor for supplementary materials. Slow or special needs learners have unlimited, free access to special materials and live support.

The home-based, online learning revolution (originally facilitated by digital TV systems) has resulted in a rapid reduction of the number of old-fashioned "school factories." Colleges and universities also have disappeared or have partnered with industry and government units to provide online, post-compulsory education and vocational courses. These merged organizations now compete for a share in an international education market. Most of the old examination validation bodies are obsolete. Private companies, which provide global education and training with a brand name and market identity, evaluate their own products against governmental regulations and international standards. The boundaries of cultural identity no longer exist; they have been replaced with allegiance to a "brand" of educational products and to specific sponsors.

With the help of national attainment database records and analysis provided by artificial intelligence software, online "education brokers" select appropriate learning packages for students between the ages of 14 and 80+. Brokers use a search engine to filter the range of possible course products for any given learner. They then consult the national database, which cross-references every student's attainment records, known learning aptitudes, and educational preferences with required learning objectives and with the product data of participating course software providers. A "course product" might consist of one module from Microsoft, one from Plato, and two from Kellogg's; in combination, these modules provide the desired knowledge and skills profile. They also produce fast learning outcomes because they automatically tailor themselves to the learner's optimum learning profile.

> *The boundaries of cultural identity no longer exist; they have been replaced with allegiance to a "brand" of educational products and to specific sponsors.*

Artificial intelligence software continually monitors the learner's actions. In the process, it performs two valuable functions: (1) the software identifies optimal learning conditions in order to generate similar learning situations in the future and to avoid learning strategies that prove ineffective; and (2) it notes areas of weak achievement or knowledge, then customizes the program to include remedial material and/or to adjust the nature and speed of the delivery of instruction. The software's analysis of learning patterns and assessment data shows marked differences in the learning strategies, problem-solving techniques, and stimulus requirements of males and females. It adjusts for these differences and thus, with newly developed gender-specific online teaching materials, improves the performance of all pupils.

The national attainment database (maintained by a company in India) uses what is called a National Insurance Number as an identifier; consequently, even if a student changes his or her name or gender, his or her profile will not be compromised. Educational and training software from every learning location feeds the database. The database even analyzes, categorizes, and records the strategic planning, problem solving, and creative thinking skills that a student utilizes while playing computer games. Because the student is unsupervised when producing game-based attainment data, it generally is used only for secondary (inference) analysis purposes — unless the data is supported by the repeated demonstration of learned responses within a broad range of situations.

■ Vocational Education

Adults access vocational education and training in the same way that children access educational materials. Most professionals learn online at home; for those who do not have computer access in their residences, a nearby learning center provides legal and financial advice, access to an enhanced job information database, and the social interaction and support that encourages skills updating. Regardless of whether a professional undertakes skills updating at home or in the learning center, he/she is always free to learn on his/her own time. Short-term contract employment is standard, and most adults therefore hold several jobs simultaneously (and endure occasional periods of unemployment). Employers routinely retest the knowledge and skills of their employees; this practice fuels the retraining industry and forces workers to continuously update their skills profiles and general abilities.

Regardless of whether a professional undertakes skills updating at home or in the learning center, he/she is always free to learn on his/her own time.

Employment brokers often work for the same companies that employ education brokers; they perform similar tasks for their clients. Employment brokers consult a national attainment database, which provides an analysis of the training needs, known learning aptitudes, and preferences of the worker in question. They compare this data with the product information from participating course software providers, then choose a course product that will enable the worker to attain his/her desired knowledge and skills profile. For a small additional fee, the worker can validate — with the appropriate assessment materials — any skills that he/she already possesses.

■ Business-Oriented Culture: The Pros and Cons

Small, disparate groups of entrepreneurs now dominate a dynamic, business-oriented culture in which qualifications matter greatly; social status, age, and gender count for little; and actual performance is everything. Most professionals use more productively the time and money they once spent commuting, and many people arrange their working lives around their social needs. The multi-skilled, flexible worker can be of any age; it is common for octogenarians to work to supplement their retirement income or savings. Because professionals work online from home, mobility is a bygone concern and commuter traffic jams are almost unknown.

To some extent, an equality of educational provision exists because everyone uses the same, or at least very similar, basic learning products. Ability is the main criterion of success, but money — from a major sponsor or private means — still buys a "fast lane" to education. The rich have always had, and will always have, a broader range of choices.

> Ability is the main criterion of success, but money — from a major sponsor or private means — still buys a "fast lane" to education.

For technophobes, those unable to learn technology-related skills, and those unwilling to adapt to change, there is low-paid, unskilled work. A substantial number of people from all age groups are unskilled laborers, and theirs is a subculture that is alienated from mainstream society. Despite sustained political effort to eradicate this alienation, it remains a serious problem.

Many pundits express concerns about the involvement of industry in education and about the power that companies have over the young, the impressionable, and society in general. Multinational companies groom selected children for future employment via premium sponsorship; they distribute corporate "bounty" on the basis of commercial self-interest and promote their names through educational products and activities. Brand loyalty even has a political dimension, since companies try to convince their sponsored students and employees to support political parties that are "friendly" to particular industries.

Education has not, however, become merely preparation for employment. Many people consider learning a leisure pursuit. Moreover, many people use the online education system to communicate about commercial, social, and political issues with people in diverse fields. These contacts form loose, but often massive, partnerships of democratic decision-making.

■ Will This Learning Revolution Really Happen?

I believe that, to some extent, it already has. Schools, colleges, universities, and a very active private sector are now providing burgeoning volumes of online courseware and assessment tools for all levels of learning. See, for example:

➤ The Computer Assisted Assessment Centre, a UK-based organization that pools knowledge and expertise about computer-assisted assessment in higher education; and the Education Resource Centre, a site administered by the University of Melbourne (Australia) that lists education resources on the World Wide Web.

➤ A directory of online courses offered by educational institutions in Connecticut.

➤ Online courseware materials from PLATO and Microsoft.

➤ ZDU, an online community that teaches consumers how to use their computers more effectively and productively; Sysnet Education (Pvt.) Ltd., a company that provides multimedia and computer-based training (CBT) to network users, system administrators, and system developers; Global Knowledge, an independent information technology (IT) training provider based in the UK and Ireland; and Getting Online, a UK-based program that currently offers three free distance learning courses in information technology.

Virtual universities are rapidly taking shape. Check out:

➤ Western Governors University, University of Phoenix, Open Learning Australia, and The Open University; and

➤ The University of the Lakes (UK) and the University of the Isles (Scotland), soon to be online.

Moreover, private companies are developing wide-ranging online vocational training offerings. Take, for example, two companies in the UK: Forte and Jarvis Hotels. Forte has spent £225K on computer-based training (CBT) for employees, and Jarvis trains 5,500 staff members with CBT (Training with Technology, 1999). On both sides of the Atlantic, colleges and training centers run by private companies are in operation. And groups of skilled professionals are beginning to establish, independently of training providers, standards for the specialized qualifications that they expect employees to have.

All this change is, at the same time, both frightening and exciting. Of course, some will benefit and some will suffer from the merger of education and business. I believe, however, that the technological future that I have envisioned will liberate and empower individuals much more than it will subjugate them — and that what we are about to see is true democracy develop. These changes will prepare us, and our children, well for the rigors of the new millennium.

Source: Alan Cummings, "Via Technology to Social Change!" Technology Source, July/August 1999. Reprinted with permission of the author.

■ **References**

"Training with Technology," *Hospitality,* 1999 April, p. 27.

Author Biographies

ZANE BERGE, PH.D. is the Director of Training Systems, Instructional Systems Development Graduate Program at the University of Maryland System, UMBC Campus. His scholarship in the field of computer-mediated communication and distance education includes numerous articles, chapters, workshops and presentations. Notably are Berge's books, co-edited with Collins. First, in 1995, was a three volume set, *Computer-Mediated Communication and the Online Classroom*, that encompasses higher and distance education. Following that was a four volume set of books, *Wired Together: Computer-Mediated Communication in the K-12 Classroom*. More recently, he and Schreiber edited, *Distance Training* (1998). Berge's newest book is *Sustaining Distance Training*, (Jossey-Bass, December 2000). He consults internationally in distance education and can be reached at **berge@umbc.edu**.

DR. TOM CAREY is the Director of the Centre for Learning and Teaching Through Technology at the University of Waterloo and a Professor in Management Science. He is a Senior Associate with the TLT Group in Washington, D.C. and a co-leader of Workplace TeleLearning Research in Canada's Telelearning Network of Centres of Excellence (TL-NCE). He was one of the founders of the academic discipline of Human-Computer Interaction in Canada and is now on his "second generation" of leading developments on learning and teaching through technology. In recent years, he has also worked with an Open University (UK) team building distance learning resources, and served as Executive Director of Graduate Program Development as part of the start-up team at a new public university.

CLIFF CARMAN

Knowledge Impact is a leading provider of end-user e-learning and performance support solutions for enterprise applications such as CRM and ERP. By offering customized learning solutions that incorporate a company's business processes, Knowledge Impact significantly increases the return on investment companies receive from their enterprise applications. Knowledge Impact's premier offering KnowledgeMate, defines the next generation of e-learning by providing end-users with on-demand training and performance support while using their enterprise application.

For nearly 20 years, Knowledge Impact has been providing solutions across the globe for leading companies such as Citibank, Fidelity, Morgan Stanley Dean Witter, Compaq, Dell Computer, Xerox, Silicon Graphics, Frontier, Abbott Laboratories, Bell Atlantic, Procter & Gamble and Enterprise Rent-A-Car. The company's offerings include KnowledgeMate, web-based training (WBT), computer-based training (CBT), e-learning and performance support solutions, instructor services and change management services. Knowledge Impact is headquartered in Wayland, MA with offices across North America. For more information, contact Knowledge Impact at **1-800-852-1230** or visit the company's web site at **www.kimpact.com**.

KATHY CARRIER is the President and owner of Training Solutions Group, LLC. She founded the firm in 1998 and provides strategic direction for the firm and works with clients in a consultative capacity. The firm provides both instructional design and facilitation services in the traditional classroom setting and the e-learning arenas. In her 20-year career, Carrier has managed audit engagements for a public accounting firm, and spent fifteen years in a Fortune 500 company; the final 12 as an officer. At Lincoln Life, she was the director of training, responsible for 52 professional trainers and the creation of a $4.5 million training center. She was responsible for the design and delivery of 1,200 courses annually to employees located across the U.S. and several international training initiatives. She can be reached at **kcarrier@trainingsolutionsgroup.com**.

JEFF CREIGHTON, Founder and Chairman of EduPoint.com, gained in-depth expertise in managing the challenges of continuing education for working adults when he served as Manager of Corporate Relations for Pepperdine University's School of Business and Management. Upon leaving the University, he established the Educational Consulting Group to create productive alliances between Fortune 500 companies and educational institutions. In this capacity, Creighton launched the Education/Industry Alliance in 1997 to develop dialogue around return on investment for continuing education and has developed numerous ROI models for continuing education currently in use by major employers.

In 1999, Creighton established EduPoint.com to address the needs of both corporations and higher education providers. By developing a centralized continuing education marketplace, Creighton provides learning providers with the tools they need to gain efficiencies in acquiring and enrolling students, while empowering corporations with custom marketplace solutions enabling companies to maximize their competitive advantage by streamlining the management of employee education programs and reducing costs. For more information, visit the company's web site at **www.EduPoint.com**.

ALAN CUMMINGS is a member of the faculty of Humanities Hospitality and Science Newcastle College (England) and currently teaches information technology skills to managers in the hospitality industry. He also serves NCFE (an examination body) and Newcastle College Company Ltd. as a consultant on online assessment design and production.

Cummings is a member of the Hospitality Technology Association (HITA). His main interests are online assessment research and online distance learning facilities. He currently is researching the ability of computers to sign speech for the deaf. He can be reached at **acummings@ncl-coll.ac.uk**.

MARK DONOVAN is the former Director of UWired and Associate Director of the University of Washington's Center for American Politics and Public Policy. He has a Ph.D. in Political Science and has authored numerous articles on politics, teaching, and technology and the book *Taking Aim: Target Populations and the Wars on* AIDS *and Drugs* (Georgetown University Press, 2001). A former principle in webStrategic, he currently works for RealNetworks. He can be reached at **mdonovan@real.com**.

THOMAS J. FALKOWSKI, Vice President of Learning Strategy for click2learn.com, is responsible for defining and communicating click2learn's unique "learning approach." In that capacity, Falkowski chairs click2learn's Learning Council and Customer Council. Additionally, he leads the click2learn Strategic Consulting Group, which helps organizations use learning technologies to capture, configure, distribute and leverage intellectual capital in ways never before possible providing virtually unlimited reach and scalability. For more information, visit the company's web site at **www.click2learn.com**.

GARY GATIEN, a member of the staff of the University of Michigan, office of the chief information officer, specializes in market research and issue analysis. He previously worked as a business planner for the Information Technology Division of the University and participated in strategic planning. Gatien is the project manager and lead writer for the CIO Web site; the author, editor and project manager of the University's "Profile of IT at the University of Michigan", and the author of recent faculty and student surveys. He can be reached at **ggatien@umich.edu**.

BRANDON HALL, leading researcher, has more than 20 years of experience in research, writing, advising and presenting in corporate training. He is the editor of the *Technology for Learning* newsletter and has been a contributing editor to the American Society for Training and Development's (ASTD) *Training and Development Magazine* and a columnist for *Inside Technology Training*. Hall participates regularly as a keynote speaker in conferences such as ASTD, Online Learning and Learning Technology. Hall earned a doctorate in educational psychology and has served on the faculty of San Francisco State University's Multimedia Studies Program. He can be reached at **www.brandonhall.com**.

BARRY HOWARD, formerly the Director of Computer & Distance Learning Centers for the Bell Atlantic Corporation, is now a member of QED Consulting, a New York-based organization that specializes in human resource change management where he assists other Corporations in their transition to learning technology. He was the Director of General Electric's Computer Training School in New York and is an Adjunct Professor in Computer Science at Baruch College in New York City. He has also taught college level Management and Marketing courses using two-way video for the Center for Distance Learning (State University of New York). He can be reached at **Ceec2000@aol.com**.

JOHN G. KELLY is a senior consultant with Towers Perrin's Administrative Technology Consulting Group. Kelly is a recognized thought leader in using emerging technology effectively in Human Resources and payroll. John is frequent speaker and authored numerous articles on HRMS, benefits and technology topics. He has taught computer science and HRMS at Northeastern University, the University of California at San Diego and at San Diego State University. John has help many organizations effect change accompanying the adoption of new processes or technology. He can be reached at **kellyj@towers.com**.

NANCY LEVENBURG is presently a professor in the Marketing Department at Grand Valley State University in Grand Rapids, Michigan. She has taught courses delivered via Internet for University of California, Los Angeles (UCLA), and in the MS in Education with an Option in Online Teaching and Learning program at California State University-Hayward. She can be reached at **LevenbuN@gvsu.edu**.

BOB LOLLER is the AVP of HR Development at Phoenix Home Life Mutual Insurance Company based in Hartford, Connecticut. With a focus on performance consulting, classroom and media training and custom education interactions, his team is charged with providing learning experiences to employees to ensure their job success. Previous to this position, he was the Technical Education Director at Phoenix for three years. He has also spent the last eight years serving in various IHRIM leadership capacities, including vice-chair of the association since January 2000. He was recently reelected to serve in that capacity through December 2001. He can be reached at **robert_loller@phl.com**.

SCOTT MACKLIN is the Director of the Program for the Educational Transformation Through Technology. PETTT seeks to enhance the effectiveness of the educators at University of Washington, and thus of the institution itself, by creating a campus framework to promote the thoughtful exploration, development, assessment and dissemination of next-generation technologies and strategies for teaching and learning.

Trained in philosophy and aesthetics, Scott holds a M.Phil F from the Institute for Christian Studies, Toronto, Canada. He has worked on multimedia productions in various sectors in addition to education; including: CSPAN, Pacific Interactive which produced "Bill Nye the Science Guy, Stop the Rock" CD-ROM and commercial design and Web development at Spangler Associates. He can be reached at **smacklin@u.washington.edu**.

HOWARD MAJOR is President of Distance Learning Dynamics, a distance learning consulting and training firm. A prior Director of Distance Education, he teaches graduate education and library science courses at Eastern Michigan University. He oversees organizational development and implementation of interactive television distance education systems. A past president of Educational Teleconsortium of Michigan, Major is considered one of the nation's foremost authorities in two-way interactive television. He can be reached at **HowardT908@aol.com**.

JOHN MARTIN is Vice President of global operations for Pathlore of Columbus, Ohio, an e-Learning management system provider. John's career in online learning spans the life of the industry. He joined Pathlore's predecessor Goal Systems as a mainframe training author 18 years ago and rounded out his knowledge with positions in tech support, marketing, systems engineering and project management. He now leads Pathlore's global operations, spearheading the effort to customize Web-based learning solutions. John draws inspiration from his equally rounded personal life: He has a family (including nine dogs), a master's in philosophy and a yen for triathlons. He can be reached at **jmartin@PATHLORE.com**.

LYNNE MEALY is currently the Chief Knowledge Officer at IHRIM, Inc. She has over 17 years experience in human resources with a focus on HR information systems, compensation and strategic management. Lynne has a Master's in Library and Information Science from Rutgers University, New Brunswick, NJ, and an MBA from Suffolk University, Boston, MA. Lynne served over nine years on the IHRIM Association Board of Directors, including holding the office of President. In 1999, she was awarded IHRIM's highest honor, the Summit Award. She can be reached at **lmealy@bellatlantic.net**.

JAMES MORRISON received his Ph.D. at the Florida State University in 1969. He moved to The University of North Carolina at Chapel Hill as associate professor of education in 1973 and was promoted to full professor in 1977. At UNC he teaches courses in research, planning, management and using technology in educational organizations. He founded *On the Horizon* and currently serves as editor emeritus. With James Ptaszynski, he co-founded and currently serves as editor of *The Technology Source* (**http://horizon.unc.edu/TS/**). He can be reached at **morrison@unc.edu**.

CHARLES MORRISSEY is a 30-year veteran of the instructional software field. He founded a pioneering company in this field in 1966, an alliance with the famous

Dartmouth BASIC language project. Houghton Mifflin Publishing Company acquired this venture in 1978. Subsequently, he became an interim CEO for two software companies in California before entering the management education field at the University of California-Irvine's Graduate School of Management where he taught from 1984-1989. He joined Pepperdine in 1989 where he is currently an associate professor of information systems. He can be reached at **Cmorrissey@aol.com**.

PEGGI MUNKITTRICK has been involved in connected learning since 1984 when she joined Pennsylvania's Teleteaching Project as a virtual instructor. Since that time, she has taught and administered secondary and post-secondary distance education initiatives using correspondence, audiographic, interactive video and Wweb-based technologies. She joined SCT in 1999. She can be reached at **pmunkitt@sctcorp.com**.

DIRK RODENBURG is Director of Knowledge Management for Inform Interactive. As an analyst and educational technology specialist, Dirk is responsible for the strategic and conceptual framework driving many of Inform's application development initiatives. Prior to working at Inform Interactive, Dirk worked for both the Faculty of Medicine and the Division of Educational Support and Development at the University of British Columbia as a multimedia/educational programmer. He can be reached at **Dirk@ii3.com**.

ANITA ROSEN is the co-founder and CEO of ReadyGo, Inc., specializing in quick, easy and inexpensive authoring tools for creating corporate e-learning sites. The company's premier product, ReadyGo Web Course Builder (tm) (WCB), has received praise from both analysts and press. Rosen is a successful teacher and speaker on Internet-related topics and has appeared as a guest speaker on many business radio programs, most recently The Jerry Bowyer Show, America Radio's — It's Your Money, the Edward Lowe Report and International Business on KUCI; Internet shows including: NetLibrary eBook, HomeOfficeMag.com, and STOCKUP.COM. She has been a contributing editor to the I.T.*Times*, and key note speaker for conferences given by the Country of Singapore, French Telecom and the American Management Association. Rosen is also a successful author. Her books include *eCommerce Question and Answer Book*, *Looking Into Intranets and the Internet*, *advice for managers*, and *Using Product Teams to get Products Out on Time and on Budget*. For more insormation, visit the company's web site at **www.readygo.com**.

JOSEPH SLOWINSKI is currently the Director of Technology at the Chadwick School. Throughout his career he has worked as a K-12 teacher, teacher trainer, education technology policy analyst, professional development specialist, and a researcher including experiences at Co-nect (comprehensive school reform provider specializing in technology integration and project-based learning), the North Central Regional Educational Laboratory (one of 10 education R&D labs nationwide), and IndianaUniversity. He has published nearly 40 articles and serves on the editorial review board of two international journals including: "Information Technology, Education & Society," and "Young: Nordic Journal of Youth Research." His most recent education technology articles appear in THE Journal, the WebNet Journal, First Monday, Technology Source, Techknowlogia, and From Now On. In addition to education technology, he is a regional expert specializing in the analysis of post-communist education with a concentration in Central and Eastern Europe. He can be reached at **joe.slowinski@chadwick-k12.com**.

STEVEN STAHL is currently a Courseware Designer/Instructional Technologist at Norwich University and has worked in the fields of adult education and early childhood education for 12 years. He designs and conducts training for trainers of early childhood and distance education programs, with an emphasis on dialogue, interaction, and self-discovery as replacements for lecture. He can be reached at **sstahl@together.net**.

DR. JOHN THOMPSON is a Project Manager and Research Associate with the University of Waterloo's Centre for Learning and Teaching Through Technology (LT3). He holds Master's degrees in Library Science and Environmental Studies and a PhD in Applied Cognitive Science. His Bachelor's degree was in Economics. When not attending school, he worked in a variety of jobs, with significant stints as a public library planning analyst, computer consultant, journalist and bicycle repairman. Connecting all these studies and engagements has been a desire to understand the cognitive and social factors that affect an individual's encounter with new tasks, new tools, and new practices, and to use that understanding to reduce the cognitive and social pain that such encounters often engender. He can be reached at **jtthomps@watservl.uwaterloo.ca**.

DR. BARRY WILLIS is currently the Associate Dean for Outreach Professor at the University of Idaho, College of Engineering and serves as the University's Executive Director for Distributed Learning. Prior to joining the University of Idaho in 1993, Willis served as the Statewide Director of Distance Education, Office of the Vice President for Academic Affairs and Research in the University of Alaska System. He has published several textbooks on distance learning (*Distance Education: Strategies and Tools*, 1994 and *Distance Education: A Practical Guide*, 1993) and is a contributing editor to the *Journal of Educational Technology*. He can be reached at **bwillis@uidaho.edu**.

ANN D. YAKIMOVICZ, PH.D., is President/CEO of Aprendio, Inc., a consultancy that helps companies use effective training strategies to plan, implement and measure their success in using technology for work and learning. She also teaches online courses in test design for Capella University. Prior to starting her consulting firm, she was Director of Interactive Learning Technology for Columbia/HCA Healthcare Corporation, a 347-hospital company, where she led the design, development and implementation of the first intranet-based training in the healthcare field. For more information, visit the company's web site at **www.aprendio.com**.

CHRIS ZIRKLE, PH.D., is an Assistant Professor in the Department of Industrial Technology Education at Indiana State University, Terre Haute, Indiana. He teaches two courses a semester utilizing the multiple delivery methods described in the article and is currently conducting research in the area of access barriers to distance education courses and programs. He holds a doctoral degree in education from Ohio State University and has teaching and administrative experience at the secondary and postsecondary levels. He can be reached at **C-Zirkle@indstate.edu**.

E-Learning Glossary of Terms

Asynchronous

(ASYNC) Not synchronized by a common timing signal. In asynchronous communication, each character can be transmitted at any time and is distinguished by a start bit and stop bit; in synchronous communication the start and stop bits are not needed and there is a regular time interval between transmissions. With asynchronous terminals, a transmission can be initiated at either end. (*See* **Synchronous**)

Asynchronous Learning

Asynchronous learning occurs when the students are learning independently and not necessarily on the same schedule as other students.

Audio Streaming

Playing audio immediately as it is downloaded from the Internet, rather than storing it in a file on the receiving computer first. Streaming is accomplished by way of Web browser plug-ins, which decompress and play the file in real time; a fast computer and fast connection are necessary. (*See* **Streaming** *and* **Video Streaming**)

Authoring System

A collection of tools that can be used by non-programmers to create interactive applications.

Bandwidth

The information carrying capacity of a communications channel or line; sometimes referred to as speed because digital bandwidth is measured as datarate. (In general, the higher the datarate, the higher the quality of video.)

Bulletin Board Systems (BBS)

An electronic message center. Most bulletin boards serve specific interest groups. They allow you to dial in with a modem, review messages left by others, and leave your own message if you want. Bulletin boards are a particularly good place to find free or inexpensive software products. In the United States alone, there are tens of thousands of BBSs.

Chat

Real-time communication between two users via computer. Once a chat has been initiated, either user can enter text by typing on the keyboard and the entered text will appear on the other user's monitor. Most networks and online services offer a chat feature.

Chat Room

A real-time electronic forum; a virtual room where visitors can meet others and share ideas on a particular subject. There are chat rooms on the Internet, BBSs, and other online services.

Computer Based Training (CBT)

A type of education in which the student learns by executing special training programs on a computer. CBT is especially effective for training people to learn computer applications because the CBT program can be integrated with the applications and students can practice using the application as they learn (often called simulation). Historically, CBT growth has been hampered by the enormous resources required: human resources to create a CBT program and hardware resources needed to run it. However, the increase in PC computing power, and especially the growing prevalence of computers equipped with CD-ROMs is making CBT a more viable option for corporations and individuals alike. Many PC applications now come with some modest form of CBT, often called a tutorial. CBT is also called computer-assisted instruction (CAI).

Courseware

Software designed to be used in an educational program.

Digital Whiteboard

The equivalent of a blackboard, but on a computer screen. A whiteboard allows one or more users to draw on the screen while others on the network watch, and can be used for instruction the same way a blackboard is used in a classroom.

Distance Learning or E-Learning

A type of education where students work on their own at home or at the office and communicate with faculty and other students via e-mail, electronic forums, videoconferencing and other forms of computer-based communication. Distance learning is becoming especially popular with companies that need to regularly re-train their employees because it is less expensive than bringing all the students together in a traditional classroom setting.

Most distance learning programs include a computer-based training (CBT) system and communications tools to produce a virtual classroom. Because the Internet and World Wide Web are accessible from virtually all computer platforms, they serve as the foundation for many distance learning systems.

Electronic Forums

An online discussion group. Online services and bulletin board services (BBS's) provide a variety of forums, in which participants with common interests can exchange open messages. Forums are sometimes called newsgroups (in the Internet world) or conferences.

Email or e-mail

Short for electronic mail, the transmission of messages over communications networks. The messages can be notes entered from the keyboard or electronic files stored on disk. Most mainframes, minicomputers, and computer networks have an e-mail system. Some electronic-mail systems are confined to a single computer system or network, but others have gateways to other computer systems, enabling users to send electronic mail anywhere in the world. Companies that are fully computerized make extensive use of e-mail because it is fast, flexible, and reliable.

Extranet

The extension of a company's intranet out onto the Internet, most often to allow selected customers, suppliers and mobile workers to access the company's private data and applications via the Web.

Hyperlink

An element in an electronic document that links to another place in the same document or to an entirely different document. Typically, you click on the hyperlink to follow the link. Hyperlinks are the most essential ingredient of all hypertext systems, including the World Wide Web.

Interactive CourseWare

A U.S. military term for software used with computer-aided instruction and computer-based training. Interactive CourseWare relies on interaction with the trainee to determine the pacing and sequence of a course of instruction.

Interactive Video

Video in which the user can control which part of a program to view, or interact with certain parts of the program.

internet

A network of networks; a group of networks interconnected via routers. The Internet (with a capital I) is the world's largest internet.

Internet

The biggest internet in the world. This worldwide information highway is comprised of thousands of interconnected computer networks, and reaches millions of people in many different countries.

Intranet

An in-house Web site that serves the employees of the enterprise. Although intranet pages may link to the Internet, an intranet is not a site accessed by the general public. Intranets use the same communications protocols as the Web and thus provide a standard way of disseminating information internally and extending the application worldwide at the same time.

Learning Management Systems (LMS)

A combination of software and hardware that host and manage courses and monitor employee progress.

Learnware

Education software.

LISTSERV

An automatic mailing list server. When e-mail is addressed to a LISTSERV mailing list, it is automatically broadcast to everyone on the list. The result is similar to a newsgroup or forum, except that the messages are transmitted as e-mail and are therefore available only to individuals on the list. LISTSERV is currently a commercial product marketed by L-Soft International. Although LISTSERV refers to a specific mailing list server, the term is sometimes used incorrectly to refer to any mailing list server. (*See* **Mailing List Server**)

Mailing List

An email discussion forum. Participants subscribe to a list, receive copies of messages sent by other members, and can email their own comments. In some mailing lists there is a moderator who receives all mail, screens it, and decides which messages to pass on. Unmoderated lists simply redirect all mail received to the list of recipients. Mailing lists may be highly technical, or social and recreational. The advantage of mailing lists over public Usenet groups is that the discussion is limited to highly interested and committed participants, and therefore more focused.

Mailing List Server

A server that manages mailing lists for groups of users.

Multimedia

The use of computers to present text, graphics, video, animation, and sound in an integrated way. Long touted as the future revolution in computing, multimedia applications were, until the mid-90s, uncommon due to the expensive hardware required. With increases in performance and decreases in price, however, multimedia is now commonplace. Nearly all PCs are capable of displaying video, though the resolution available depends on the power of the computer's video adapter and CPU.

Because of the storage demands of multimedia applications, the most effective media are CD-ROMs.

Nonlinear Video

A linear video is viewed or edited in a linear sequence. CD-ROMs and LaserDiscs can display nonlinear video, in which the user can jump from frame to frame or clip to clip in any order.

Portals

Basically, a door into the Internet or a mega-Website. More specifically, a Website that aims to provide many services to its users — such as search, weather, news, content, and links to other sites. Yahoo is a perfect example of a portal.

Streaming

A technique for transferring data such that it can be processed as a steady and continuous stream. Streaming technologies are becoming increasingly important with the growth of the Internet because most users do not have fast enough access to download large multimedia files quickly. With streaming, the client browser or plug-in can start displaying the data before the entire file has been transmitted.

There are a number of competing streaming technologies emerging. For audio data on the Internet, the de facto standard is Progressive Network's RealAudio. (*See* **Audio Streaming** *and* **Video Streaming**)

Synchronous

Capable of performing two or more processes at the same time, such as sending and receiving data, using a common timing signal. (*See* **Asynchronous**)

Synchronous Learning

Synchronous learning occurs when the students are taught at the same time (although not necessarily the same place). Examples would be typical instructor-led classroom training or workshops that are broadcast to conference rooms as the event occurs.

Teleconference

To hold a conference via telephone or network connection. Computers have given new meaning to the term because they allow groups to do much more than just talk. Once a teleconference is established, the group can share applications and mark up a common whiteboard. There are many teleconferencing applications that work over private networks. One of the first to operate over the Internet is Microsoft's NetMeeting.

Videoconferencing

Conducting a conference between two or more participants at different sites by using computer networks to transmit audio and video data. For example, a point-to-point (two-person) video conferencing system works much like a video telephone. Each participant has a video camera, microphone, and speakers mounted on his or her computer. As the two participants speak to one another, their voices are carried over the network and delivered to the other's speakers, and whatever images appear in front of the video camera appear in a window on the other participant's monitor.

Multipoint videoconferencing allows three or more participants to sit in a virtual conference room and communicate as if they were sitting right next to each other.

Video Streaming

Playing video immediately as it is downloaded from the Internet, rather than storing it in a file on the receiving computer first. Streaming is accomplished by way of Web browser plug-ins, which decompress and play the file in real time; a fast computer and fast connection are necessary. (*See* **Audio Streaming** *and* **Streaming**)

Web (World Wide Web)

The World Wide Web (WWW). A hypermedia-based system for browsing Internet sites. It is named the Web because it is made of many sites linked together; users can travel from one site to another by clicking on hyperlinks. Text, graphics, sound, and video can all be accessed with browsers like Mosaic, Netscape, or Internet Explorer. The Web can also be accessed with text-only browsers like Lynx.

Sources: AOL *Webopedia -* http://aol.pcwebopedia.com/ *and ComputerUser High-Tech Dictionary -* http://www.computeruser.com/resources/dictionary

International
Association for
Human Resource
Information Management

IHRIM's (The International Association for Human Resource Information Management) mission is to be the leading global source of knowledge for the application of human resource information and technology to improve organizational effectiveness. Achievement of this mission comes from the delivery of a wide variety of products and services offered to customers around the globe. One of IHRIM's newest products is a book series focusing on a variety of topics that benefit the entire HR community. This particular book, the third in the series, addresses the growing field of e-learning and its impact on the way people learn.

Learning is about people sharing information. The Internet and intranets facilitate that learning in a 24/7 environment. E-learning will not replace the classroom nor bring an end to people getting together to share knowledge. But e-learning can enhance knowledge-sharing in today's global business environment, and this collection of articles from some of the field's experts has something of interest for every HR discipline.

We hope you enjoy the book and invite you to order one or more books and periodicals from IHRIM Press. For more information about publications, membership, conferences, education, and other programs, visit **www.ihrim.org**, e-mail **more-info@ihrim.org**, or call **+1.312.321.5141**.

Sincerely,

B. Lynn DeLeo
Chairman of the Board and President
International Association for Human
Resource Information Management

Other IHRIM Publications

■ *21 Tomorrows: HR Systems in the Emerging Workplace of the 21st Century*

Edited by Robert H. Stambaugh

The first in a series of IHRIM books, 21 *Tomorrows* is a collection of original essays by HRIS thought leaders. The authors address new systems, people and management challenges we will all confront in the 21st century HRIS environments. The chapters provide the short- and long-term predictions that practitioners will need to make sense of what's happening in our industry today — and tomorrow. The book is available to IHRIM members for **US$29** — a discount of US$10.00 off the cover price.

■ *Knowledge Management: Clarifying the Key Issues*

By Scott I. Tannenbaum, Ph.D. and George M. Alliger, Ph.D.

This IHRIM book is designed to stimulate dialogue and foster a shared understanding of relevant knowledge management (KM) issues among HR professionals, information technologists and business leaders. The authors emphasize a few recurring themes that reflect their core beliefs about KM — smaller can be better, technology is not KM, start with business needs and understand the big picture. Each chapter addresses a key question and highlights a pitfall to avoid. The book is available to IHRIM members for **US$29** — a discount of US$10.00 off the cover price.

■ IHRIM.link

This bi-monthly magazine is provided as a member benefit and is available by subscription to non-members for an annual price of **US$60**. Whether you're exploring the human resource information management field as a beginner, or you're an expert thick in the trenches of its technology, the IHRIM.*link* is a significant resource. Innovative feature articles, relevant columns and case histories as well as current marketplace news are found in each issue.

■ IHRIM Journal

Published quarterly, the *Journal* is available by subscription only; **US$70** to IHRIM members and **US$120** to non-members. The *Journal* is written by recognized experts in the field for current and emerging thought leaders and senior management. Each issue features global industry trends and international perspectives, engaging readers to think in strategic business terms and position themselves in writing the new rules of fast-changing business.

These publications may be ordered online at www.ihrim.org or by calling 1.312.321.5141. Watch for more IHRIM publications throughout 2001.